Praise for Design Leadership

"Design is quickly becoming a sustainable competitive advantage, and Design Leadership a sorely sought after skill. This book is a great distillation of the experiences of some of the top digital design leaders around the world and is required reading whether you're already one of those leaders or you simply aspire to be."

—Martin Eriksson, Cofounder, Curator and Editor of Mind the Product

"An alternate title for this great book could easily be 'Expert Advice for Design Managers on How to Become a Design Leader... and Bring Your Company Along with You.'"

—Tom Hughes, Cofounder of Idealab

"If you're running a creative team, ignore this book at your peril."

—Andrew Wilkinson, Founder of MetaLab

"This book is a must-read for designers looking to take their leadership skills to the next level. It is not a how-to book, but something more rare: a powerful collection of advice from experienced design leaders. Richard Banfield's interviews, combined with his personal experience in the field, provide a wealth of both information and inspiration."

—Andy Pratt, Executive Creative Director of Favorite Medium; Coauthor of Interactive Design: An Introduction to the Theory and Application of User-centered Design

Design Leadership

How Top Design Leaders Build and Grow Successful Organizations

Richard Banfield

Beijing · Boston · Farnham · Sebastopol · Tokyo

Design Leadership

by Richard Banfield

Published by O'Reilly Media, Inc., 1005 Gravenstein Highway North, Sebastopol, CA 95472.

O'Reilly books may be purchased for educational, business, or sales promotional use. Online editions are also available for most titles (*http://safaribooksonline.com*). For more information, contact our corporate/institutional sales department: 800-998-9938 or *corporate@oreilly.com*.

Editor: Angela Rufino
Acquisitions Editor: Nick Lombardi
Production Editor: Shiny Kalapurakkel
Copyeditor: Gillian McGarvey
Proofreader: Christina Edwards

Indexer: Ellen Troutman
Interior Designer: David Futato
Cover Designer: Karen Montgomery
Illustrator: Rebecca Demarest

December 2015:   First Edition

Revision History for the First Edition
2015-12-03:   First Release

See *http://oreilly.com/catalog/errata.csp?isbn=9781491929209* for release details.

978-1-491-92920-9

[LSI]

Contents

Preface

Why I Wrote This Book and for Whom

Somehow we've convinced our leaders that they need to have all the answers. We've elevated company leadership to an almost mythological state of knowing everything and never making mistakes. The reality is that all leaders, including product and website design leaders, are just as confused as everyone else. They make mistakes. They screw up. They make things up along the way. They forget lessons and lose direction. In surveys for this book, almost 50% of design leaders said they are merely "reasonable leaders and still have tons to learn," and only 13% consider themselves to be "very good" leaders. Considering that these are the people in charge of the top design companies in North America, it's confirmation that even the smartest and most experienced leaders struggle with the challenges of leadership.

This book was written partly out of personal frustration and partly because there's a lot of misunderstanding about what *design leadership* means. Leading a successful digital design organization is confusing and challenging. There's no definitive manual or guidebook. The unhealthy perception that leaders have all the answers makes leaders less likely to ask for help. That's a perception that can only lead to disappointment for both the leaders and those who look to them for direction. Design leaders need better guidance and insight. This book aims to provide some of that knowledge.

I'm one of those confused design leaders. I've been an entrepreneur in the tech and digital design space for most of my adult life. That's about 20 years, in case you're wondering. In that time, I've learned the hard way that nobody has all the answers. I've also learned that as a leader, you can either find the answers through trial and error or you can go directly to the source. I prefer going to the source. If you want to know how to be a great design leader, go directly to the best design leaders. When I started my own design firm, Fresh Tilled Soil, 10 years ago, there were lots of questions. Questions with no obvious answers. For a while I believed I was supposed to learn the answers the hard way, through trial and error. Over time I learned that this was inefficient and expensive. I endeavored to read about how other leaders had solved these problems but the published answers seemed a little too generic. The real breakthroughs came when I had the opportunity to talk directly to other design leaders who were more experienced and smarter than me. These conversations inspired me to create a successful strategy for myself, which allowed me to grow a multimillion-dollar design company from the ground up with no debt and outside investors. These conversations were so helpful that I made a regular habit of calling design leaders that were way ahead of me on their personal and business journeys and asking for their advice.

I noticed that I wasn't the only one who was asking questions. These topics came up frequently during conferences, industry meetings, and casual conversations. It started to make sense to capture these conversations and gather all these perspectives and answers into a book. I imagined that what was useful to me could also be useful to other design leaders. So, to that end, this book was born.

This book is both for established design leaders and for those on the path to leadership. The book will also be useful to people who work for design leaders and want to understand them better. Ultimately, the book is for anyone who leads a design team, owns an emerging design company, or works closely with design leaders. Whether you're starting out or are decades deep into your adventure, this book will guide you through topics like hiring the best talent, building a strong culture, finding personal balance, growing your leadership skills, designing the optimal workspace, and creating healthy sales pipelines.

We interviewed leaders from emerging and established companies. In the cases where the design firm was independently owned and run by the design leader, we focused on companies in the 5 to 100 employees range. There were some exceptions, but our goal was to talk to leaders dealing with typical growing pains. Although we did speak to leaders from larger corporations like ESPN and Fidelity Investments, we gave most of our attention to small- and mid-sized design teams. About 60% of the companies interviewed had between 5 and 15 employees, while almost 40% of the companies had 20 or more employees. Several had upwards of 75 team members. The cultural differences between these companies is enormous and it would be hard to quantify those differences.

Instead we've captured the individual stories, universal insights, and strategic approaches to making design groups more productive, creative, and focused.

This book is not a textbook or a paint-by-numbers workbook. This book is a conversation. It is a collection of conversations teased out of hundreds of interviews that I did with the help of my colleague and friend, Dan Allard. Dan was one of the first employees at Fresh Tilled Soil and is just as curious about design leadership as I am. While I conducted the interviews, Dan lugged around the heavy video and audio equipment to dozens of cities across North America. We recorded almost a hundred design leader interviews, ranging from small companies like Haught Codeworks in Boulder, CO, to massive corporations like ESPN with its 120-acre campus in Bristol, CT. From late-2013 until mid-2015, we captured the perspectives, insights, anecdotes, and personal stories of some of the top digital design leaders in North America. Many of these original interviews are available on YouTube in their raw and unedited form. Just search for "digital design leader" and you'll find dozens of one-on-one interviews to inspire you. Over the last two years, some of this footage has found its way into podcasts and articles, but this book will be the first time all the interviews are collected into a single publication.

I hope you enjoy reading this book as much as I've enjoyed creating it. I've learned so much from my interactions with these leaders and I hope you will, too. Getting to know them so intimately has also led to some great friendships and even a few partnerships. With the help of my editors, reviewers, and publishers, I tried to make the writing clear and engaging. We deliberately avoided making this a prescriptive manual for running a design organization. Instead, we curated the "best of breed" approaches and presented them in a way that allows you to decide what works best for your team. Our goal was to cover the subject matter comprehensively but not in such detail that it puts you to sleep. No matter what your design leadership position or aspirations are, we are quite sure you will find something valuable in this book.

We'd also like to continue this conversation with our readers and contributors on social media and in person. As I've said before, design leaders don't have all the answers, and we know there's loads more to explore and learn. Let's work together to get smarter and spread the knowledge so we can all benefit. A rising tide raises all boats. The more informed we are as design leaders, the sooner our organizations will see results. The more we share, the more we'll see highly engaged teams, happy clients, and positive financial returns.

Thank you for buying and reading this book. It's been a real pleasure writing it and sharing it with so many other design leaders.

—*Richard Banfield*

How This Book Is Organized

CHAPTER 1: CULTURE

As the investor Jonathan Beare once said to me, "Every company has its own brand of culture and politics. You have to figure out which culture and politics are most interesting to you." This chapter explores the way design leaders create and nurture the culture in their successful organizations. We'll hear from design studio owners and executives about the links between culture, attracting talent, productivity, and purpose.

CHAPTER 2: TALENT

People are the cornerstone of all organizations. Great people make great organizations. Finding these people and keeping them engaged and happy is one of the primary responsibilities of design leaders. We'll explore the innovative ways these leaders attract and nurture talent in their organizations.

CHAPTER 3: OFFICE SPACE AND REMOTE WORKING

Today's workspace looks nothing like your dad's office did 20 years ago. Walls are coming down and creative workers are more remote than ever. In this chapter we ask top design leaders what makes their design studios deliver on the promise of being productive spaces for team members and clients. We also ask them how they manage the increasing numbers of remote workers while maintaining strong cultural bonds between team members.

CHAPTER 4: PERSONAL GROWTH AND FINDING BALANCE

Design leaders are always learning, growing, and struggling with finding balance in their lives. We learned how these top performers find time to stay on top of their daily demands while not losing sight of what's really important—family, friends, and personal growth. There is no one-size-fits-all approach either. We find out how different personalities solve this universal problem with their own brand of intuition and creativity.

CHAPTER 5: PLANNING FOR THE FUTURE

The ambiguity of running a design studio or team is becoming increasingly hard. Quickly changing tech trends demand agility and flexibility from leaders. Planning for a future that seems to change by the minute requires leadership skills that are both strategic and tactical. Our design leaders describe how they are laying plans for the future while consistently delivering on today's demands.

CHAPTER 6: LEADERSHIP STYLES

Each person we interviewed brings their own flavor and style to the art of leadership. No two styles are the same, but there are patterns that are consistent with successful leaders. We discuss how these styles connect leaders to their business visions and company cultures. Over time, design leaders adapt their styles to changing environments and new challenges.

CHAPTER 7: SALES AND MARKETING

Every design business needs a pipeline of work. This topic is foremost on the design leaders' minds as they work through the challenges of attracting new clients and retaining existing clients. Our interviews gave us insight into companies big and small, and provided us with a wide range of techniques and approaches.

CHAPTER 8: LEARNING FROM OUR BIGGEST MISTAKES

Making mistakes is inevitable. Unfortunately, learning from them is not. We delve into the mistakes that these great design leaders have made and what they did to bounce back from them. In these stories, you'll learn that making mistakes isn't something to be avoided; rather, having mechanisms to grow and improve as a result of mistakes is what makes design leaders great.

COMPANIES INTERVIEWED FOR THIS BOOK

Teehan+Lax
Happy Cog
Virgin Pulse
LogMeIn
Fidelity Investments
The Program
Make
XPLANE
America's Test Kitchen
eHouse Studio

Envy

ESPN

SuperFriendly

The Working Group

Uncorked Studios

Forrester Research

Kore Design

Yellow Pencil

Plank

Velir

Plucky

Fastspot

Demac Media

BancVue

BigCommerce

Funsize

Zurb

Viget

The Grommet

Barrel

Fresh Tilled Soil

Haught Codeworks

Crowd Favorite

Grey Interactive

Think Brownstone

nGen Works

Digital of Bureau

Mechanica

Planantir

ACKNOWLEDGMENTS

This book would not be possible without the tireless efforts of Dan Allard. As we crisscrossed North America interviewing design leaders, Dan was the camera-man, soundman, and general Sherpa of all the equipment. I'd also like to thank the entire Fresh Tilled Soil team for holding down the fort while I researched and wrote this book. I'd also like to recognize the Bureau of Digital founders, Greg Hoy and Carl Smith, who host the amazing Owner Camp retreats. Meeting them and the fellow campers was a tipping point in getting access to several of the design leaders interviewed here. Finally, I'd like to thank Nick Lombardi, Angela Rufino, and the rest of the amazing team at O'Reilly whose attention to detail and dedication make writing a book so much more enjoyable.

Conventions Used in This Book

The following typographical conventions are used in this book:

Tip

This element signifies a tip or suggestion.

Note

This element signifies a general note.

Warning

This element indicates a warning or caution.

Using Code Examples

This book is here to help you get your job done. In general, if example code is offered with this book, you may use it in your programs and documentation. You do not need to contact us for permission unless you're reproducing a significant portion of the code. For example, writing a program that uses several chunks of code from this book does not require permission. Selling or distributing a CD-ROM of examples from O'Reilly books does require permission. Answering a question by citing this book and quoting example code does not require permission. Incorporating a significant amount of example code from this book into your product's documentation does require permission.

We appreciate, but do not require attribution. An attribution usually includes the title, author, publisher, and ISBN. For example: *Design Leadership* by Richard Banfield (O'Reilly). Copyright 2016 Richard Banfield, 978-1-4919-2920-9."

If you feel your use of code examples falls outside fair use or the permission given above, feel free to contact us at *permissions@oreilly.com*.

Safari® Books Online

 Safari Books Online is an on-demand digital library that delivers expert *content* in both book and video form from the world's leading authors in technology and business.

Technology professionals, software developers, web designers, and business and creative professionals use Safari Books Online as their primary resource for research, problem solving, learning, and certification training.

Safari Books Online offers a range of plans and pricing for enterprise, government, education, and individuals.

Members have access to thousands of books, training videos, and prepublication manuscripts in one fully searchable database from publishers like O'Reilly Media, Prentice Hall Professional, Addison-Wesley Professional, Microsoft Press, Sams, Que, Peachpit Press, Focal Press, Cisco Press, John Wiley & Sons, Syngress, Morgan Kaufmann, IBM Redbooks, Packt, Adobe Press, FT Press, Apress, Manning, New Riders, McGraw-Hill, Jones & Bartlett, Course Technology, and hundreds more. For more information about Safari Books Online, please visit us online.

How to Contact Us

Please address comments and questions concerning this book to the publisher:

O'Reilly Media, Inc.
1005 Gravenstein Highway North
Sebastopol, CA 95472
800-998-9938 (in the United States or Canada)
707-829-0515 (international or local)
707-829-0104 (fax)

We have a web page for this book, where we list errata, examples, and any additional information. You can access this page at *http://oreil.ly/1jyLP2n*.

To comment or ask technical questions about this book, send email to *bookquestions@oreilly.com*.

For more information about our books, courses, conferences, and news, see our website at *http://www.oreilly.com*.

Find us on Facebook: *http://facebook.com/oreilly*
Follow us on Twitter: *http://twitter.com/oreillymedia*
Watch us on YouTube: *http://www.youtube.com/oreillymedia*

Culture

Introduction

The elusive nature of company culture is what makes it both fascinating and frustrating. The role culture plays in the success of a design team can't be quantified but is so significant that every leader we spoke to put it at the top of their list. Knowing how to design, nurture, curate, or even change culture seems like one of the greatest challenges of a growing company. In this chapter, we learn how leaders create and nurture a positive culture in their organizations.

In our conversations with leaders, we were interested to learn that many leaders don't deliberately set out to create a particular culture. Instead, they provide a space for it to develop on its own—in a sense, acting like good parents: providing guidance and setting boundaries while allowing the culture to maintain its independence and develop its own personality. Even in the larger organizations and studios we visited, there was a feeling that the culture had a life of its own and the leadership was there to gently guide it along.

Being such a universal leadership topic, it made sense to start off the book talking about culture. This book doesn't suggest what type of culture is the best or worst. Different cultures are just like the people that create them. Diversity in cultures is what makes the world go round. Trying to prescribe one generic cultural style to fit all design organizations is unnecessary and unhelpful.

We were mostly interested in the "why" behind culture as a strategic advantage for our design leaders. We wanted to know why they cared about culture. Our inquiry was into how leaders approached this subject to create the best possible culture for their specific organizations. Obviously there are generalizations about transparency, diversity, open communication, and supportive team structures that can be drawn from these observations, but the reasons for these patterns are more important than the patterns themselves. This chapter focuses on reasons to give culture your attention and how these deliberate efforts lead to positive outcomes.

It Starts with the People

Successful culture has many benefits. The one most frequently mentioned by our design leaders is the connection between a positive culture and the acquisition and retention of great talent. If a rewarding and supportive culture can be sustained, then culture can also have a strong influence on developing good chemistry between team members. The genesis of positive culture starts when the team is aligned with the inherent values and guiding vision of the organization. This bonding between people and the company vision gives culturally healthy companies an edge in several areas, not the least of which is that strongly aligned firms are attractive not only to design talent but to prospective clients. Design leaders agree that a strong culture plays directly into easier hiring, increased productivity, and overall job satisfaction. In one survey, 70% of our leaders stated that culture was "very important" to their company's success.

On the other end of the spectrum, companies that lack a strong culture tend to be characterized by a lack of loyalty, issues with trust, little or no diversity, misaligned goals, and poor communication. Anthony and Natalie Armendariz, who together run Funsize in Austin agree. "We've been lucky enough to not have any turnover, in terms of someone wanting to leave. Turnover of staff is probably our biggest fear and something we work the hardest to try not to have. The culture here is the most important thing. The culture is number one." Even though Funsize is only a few years old, they have prioritized culture from the beginning. Culture comes first at Funsize, and this level of interest in culture is tangible when you visit their office. Armendariz proudly walks around their office introducing us to every person and describing each detail of their space. His commitment to the team's well-being is contagious.

In a talent marketplace characterized by signing bonuses and generous benefits, smaller agencies like Funsize have fewer resources to offer when competing for talent. They make up for that by providing flexible time and more intimacy with the business decisions. "We can't be as competitive as some of the other agencies are in terms of salary, but what we can do is make sure that people are working on great products that they're going to be proud of, on projects that they are excited about, and have a very high caliber portfolio versus their peers," explains Armendariz. "We provide the opportunity to lead, to be involved in business decisions, and to manage their work hours. We work Monday through

Thursday, meaning that we don't work any of our designers more than 32 hours a week, and based on the teams we've put together recently, I'd say the average person is ... working 24 to 32 hours a week."

Requiring so few hours was not something we came across very often in our interviews, but as we'll see in other chapters, the number of hours spent at work doesn't correlate with productivity. Time working together seems to be far more important than the time captured in the time-tracking tools. Even larger agencies use time-specific or time-related activities as a cultural bonding opportunity. Neil McPhedran, General Manager at Gray in Vancouver, points out how time connects their people. "We used to have a weekly status where we would spend a good hour and a half working through it and that was it. I've moved us towards more agile project management, so with a daily huddle at 9:17 a.m. we stand up and we do a quick round-the-horn of what everyone's doing, and the idea is that we're all responsible for our own things and we know that." Quick, smart meetings like this one were frequently mentioned when we visited design firms and influenced the company culture from the bottom up.

McPhedran was clear that his primary goal in these meetings is to help his team get the most out of their day. By starting their day with an objective in mind, the teams are able to make each day a little more productive and enjoyable. This rippled through the organization and set the cultural tone for the team. "I can help people manage their time. I can hear a creative guy talking about doing this, this, this, and this and say no, you're not doing all of that, it's just impossible for you to do all of those, you can do this. Let's help everyone out. Let's prioritize. It's a way that people can take ownership of their day, but it's also a way that we can be accountable to each other. It's been great, I think—a tremendous thing for us." The daily or weekly activities allow the leadership to actively support their team's best use of time. This guidance to the team's day may seem insignificant, but it is a critical part of culture.

CULTURE TRICKLES DOWN FROM THE FOUNDERS

It's clear to us that people are the core of any design culture. It follows that the founders are the people who will have the biggest influence on that culture—for better and worse. The personal characteristics of the founders or leaders will undoubtedly find their way into the culture of a business. "I don't know if this is going to be a popular concept or not, but I think that when you are a founder or you have a couple of founders of an organization, you put a pretty strong imprint on that organization," says Dave Gray of XPLANE. "You put your strengths, your weaknesses, and all your foibles into that organization whether you realize it or not."

"There are a few of my influences for sure," says Sarah Tesla at Make in Vancouver. "I'm into adventure traveling. I love food. I love art," Tesla says as she points to the art gallery that makes up about a quarter of the entire design studio at Make. "I feel like a lot of the people here share some of those similar interests. We're a big dog culture, so we have that going on. And we had a dog trainer come in and train three or four of the puppies that were here at one point. And a few of the team members do aerobics in the space after work. So there's just little things." Not all companies will feel the need to have art galleries in their studios or dog-friendly offices, but whether intentional or not, they will borrow from the leadership's personalities and preferences.

"We're deeply rooted in geek culture and also in open source, and so that tends to provide a bit of cultural shorthand," says Tiffany Farriss, co-CEO at Palantir. "But we work really hard because inclusiveness and diversity are very important to us." Building a welcoming and inclusive culture also has the benefit of providing a level playing field so that everyone has an opportunity to advance. "It takes a sustained effort to make sure that you have that and so what we're focused on is—right now our initiative is around a culture of feedback. Being able to provide really actionable, direct, and timely feedback at any level to anyone on the project."

Our conversations confirmed that successful leaders are always actively involved in curating and communicating the culture. It's not something left to chance. Sometimes these communications are formal, but most often they are subtle. The important thing is that they are communicated regularly. Leaving culture to emerge on its own in a vacuum appears to be something that successful design leaders don't think is a good idea. Companies that communicate their vision, values, and cultural policies more frequently are more likely to have a shared agenda. This translates to shared outcomes and happier teams. Happier teams lead to a positive culture.

SAFE AND HAPPY SPACES

We asked Tracey Halvorsen, President and Chief Visionary Officer at FastSpot, what her process was in creating a positive culture, and more specifically if she saw it as something that developed on its own or if she had an idea of what she wanted it to look like. "It has to develop because as time goes by, people change. You add new people to the dynamic and you change. I always knew that I wanted a culture that was very respectful, where everyone felt like they could do their best work. A bonus would be if everyone got along and had a lot of fun, too. I think, otherwise, it's a job—but you want it to be a great job because you want people to stay."

Tracey's insight is a cornerstone to the success we saw in companies with positive cultures: there is a virtuous circle between rewarding work and happy teams. Work doesn't always have to be fun, but the team should feel respected and acknowledged. Building a safe place for your team to be creative and do their best work might be the most useful thing a leader can do for culture in design-focused organizations.

There is a subtlety to this: culture cannot only be linked to being a fun place to work. Making the assumption that an expensive office space and free lunches can buy culture is a mistake. "I guess you can force culture by doing certain things, but putting a foosball table in a room doesn't create culture," points out Warren Wilansky of Plank in Montreal. "Taking people to a restaurant doesn't create culture. Culture is created by the people in the room at that time. If you have a room of people who are nonpolitical and have each other's backs, that is going to be the company culture. And that's the way we are." Wilansky makes a very critical point about culture: it's all about the type of people in your organization. All businesses are a product of their founder's personality and the people those leaders initially hired. This influence can be both positive and negative.

"Every time you do things as a group, you're creating culture. Good culture or bad culture," Dave Gray, President of XPLANE, reminds us. "Anytime you do stuff with other people, you're creating culture. And in an organization where you're spending so much time with each other, especially in a smaller firm like a design firm, it's like your family. They know your positives and your negatives. For example, one of the things that I imprinted in my organization very early on was a love of process and a rigor in terms of process. Even today, when I'm relatively hands-off and not really involved in day-to-day operations, I can still see the results of that process-oriented culture."

PERSONALITY AS CULTURE

It's apparent that hiring a certain type of person will result in a certain type of culture. At Plank, Warren Wilansky says, "We've generally hired more introverted people and that's a little bit more my personality." We noticed that leaders in all design firms often hire people that share their values and approach to work. This creates a company culture that mirrors the founder's personality in some way. Our interviews didn't expose us to any failed cultures, but it seems obvious that toxic values will lead to toxic cultures. Of course, cultures may change or evolve as the company grows and as new people join the company because these new personalities bring different ideas and influences to the culture—that is, unless there is an ongoing and deliberate attempt to guide the culture.

Many of the design leaders we met had already shared insights into their company cultures on their blogs and in articles. The way these successful studios or teams share their cultural experiments with the public is a cultural element in itself. "We are incredibly transparent and open about what we're doing and why we're doing it," says Jason Grigsby of CloudFour in Portland, OR. "Culture's becoming this really loaded word in our society—or in our industry—and I didn't even realize how loaded it was. We used to talk about culture and trying to find cultural fit and things of that nature. And now, I'm reticent to talk about it because there are so many other places where their description of culture is basically code for trying to find like-minded people and have them work crazy hours and all that stuff. That's not us at all."

Grigsby describes the culture at CloudFour as if to ward off any bad cultural spirits. "People come in at a reasonable hour and what's reasonable varies, depending on what's going on for them. Everybody works from home on Wednesdays and people just collaborate and do work. That's the main thing that we're focused on: how do we enable that collaboration? How do we make sure that people are working well together?" Building a safe and happy space that facilitates creative work is an essential factor in a design leader's agenda, but "safe and happy" looks different to each company. Grisgsby add, "The last job position we posted was really interesting. The one thing we wrote in it was, 'We're not interested in startup insanity,' and it really resonated with a bunch of people who were looking for the position. We spent a lot of time actually working on the language to try to make sure that it was inclusive and that we would get diversity of candidates and things like that. That attention to detail actually made a difference in the candidates that we received."

For some companies, a safe place means having a culture that extends beyond the office. This can feel a little bit like the tech startup world where leadership doesn't distinguish between time at work and time at play. We heard stories where the CEO invited everybody to go to his house in a resort town for a weekend for bonding and drinking. For a lot of people that have children, those types of excursions are not options. We can't say whether this extension of culture is a good thing or a bad thing. What we can say is that any consistent activity that isn't inclusive of the whole company can send the wrong message. Having a consistent foundation from which culture can develop is like having a set of values for your business to lean on.

Laying the Foundation for Culture

At Teehan+Lax, they had a very clear idea of the foundation on which they wanted to build their company.[1] Jon Lax says, "Geoff (cofounder) and I wanted to start a company where we would want to work. When we asked ourselves what we enjoyed doing, one of the conclusions we came to very early on was that we wanted to make the work that we did the centerpiece." He continues, "What we value above all other things is the work that we do. We want to do work that is interesting. We want to do work that we think people are going to use."

Lax goes on to describe the motivation for putting the work at the center of their company culture. "I know for myself—and I'm sure Geoff would say something similar, and all the principals here would have a similar story—the charge that I felt the first time I coded a web page in 1994, put it up, checked the log file, and saw that about 100 people had looked at it, had used it, had accessed it—I think I've been chasing that dragon ever since."

Having such a strong foundation on which to build a company is going to have an ongoing effect on the emerging culture, which will develop around these leaders' clear vision for the business. Lax told us, "We decided that the value of this company wouldn't be about profit maximization. It wouldn't be about aspiring to have global offices. I'm not saying those are bad things. I think for different entrepreneurs and leaders, some people aspire to global domination. That's cool; it's just not what inspired or motivated us. We were happiest doing work that we thought was good work."

Through the implementation of particular behaviors, these leaders—even unwittingly—continue to influence culture. Lax and his principals keep their team focused on the work by asking themselves, "Would we stand up in a room of our peers and claim this work as our own? Would we be proud to say that we worked on this? If the answer is no, we go back and figure out why not."

By maintaining a close focus on their motivations for producing functional work they could be proud of, the leadership at Teehan+Lax have instilled strong values in their organization. Although, Lax acknowledges, despite having such a

---

1 Since this interview Teehan+Lax has dissolved the company. Lax and his partner Geoff Teehan have gone on to full-time design leadership positions at Facebook. Their decision to shutter the studio at the height of its growth was surprising to the design industry.

clear vision very early on, it did take them a few years to fully realize this. "The values that we started to instill in this organization, even though Geoff and I said these things to each other very early on in the business, took us a few years, and we had to look back to see that we'd created this culture where the work is the number one thing."

Our observation is that design leaders need to be conscious of what their own preferences and behaviors signal to the company as a whole. How leaders spend their time tells the rest of the team what's important and what's a low priority. This informs the culture. "On any typical day, I'm building a team so I can focus on working on design with a capital D. Inspiring and leading is how I spend my time."

DELIBERATE CULTURAL DESIGN

From our conversations and interviews, it was not always clear whether culture happened spontaneously or deliberately in successful design organizations. What *was* obvious, though, was that it wasn't ignored. It was a well-understood and thoughtfully considered part of everyday decision making. "I think that when you create a culture and you have a set of values, what you're really saying is: when I have to make decisions, I'm going to make decisions that optimize this dimension over another dimension," explains Jon Lax of Teehan+Lax. Deliberate design culture is like a good strategy—it's a vision that's held on course by a set of consistent guidelines and actions.

"For most leaders, it's an afterthought. It's not about having people follow you—it's about making people feel good about what they are doing," says Nancy Lyons, President at Clockwork. "It's not just self-help corporate marketing speak. Leadership needs to decide who they want to be internally and the rest follows organically. What are the things that we hold sacred? What are we not willing to let go? We have a corporate vocabulary that surpasses the touchy-feely stuff and that is super important." This intentional direction is consistent among successful design companies. They may not dictate every aspect of their company's culture, but they don't leave it to chance. Once they set forth the vision and guidelines, these leaders monitor the culture and nudge it back on course if it gets away from the vision.

Vince LeVecchia, cofounder of Portland-based Instrument, is pretty emphatic about how culture gets designed. "You don't create culture, you create this container and you put great people in it and you have some values and some philosophies that you run your business by—work-life balance, "work smart, play hard"—things like that, and the culture is born out of that. I really feel that the people around here create the culture and they create it organically. I can't force people to want a ping-pong tournament or to start a bowling team. All that's contrived if I'm doing it. We just put great people in the room and we see those people become friends, become partners in life, get married. Not everybody's hanging out, but a lot of people come to like each other. It's looking someone in the eye and thinking, you're going to be a great community member at Instrument, and if that's true, then the culture is created by those people."

The design leaders also connect cultural success with company success. Nancy Lyons reiterated this idea in simple terms: "The best way to create culture is to prove it with the numbers." By making culture accountable, leaders prevent it from becoming ethereal.

How leaders structure their organizations can also be part of their deliberate cultural vision. The type of culture you create is often a product of the organization you wish to create. "One of my mentors told me that you want to think about what kind of organization you are creating," says Dave Gray from XPLANE. "There's something that he called a 'membership organization' and there's something that he called a 'nurturing organization,' and they're not the same. They run differently. They operate differently." This anecdote is one of the most insightful descriptions we've heard, and helps to connect the dots between organizational structure and culture—a gap that's too often overlooked. "So let's say you have a membership organization," Gray explains. "That is the kind of organization where you have to be really, really good at the job to even get a job there; we only hire the best and if we hire you and you're not doing the best, you're out. That kind of organization is going to be very merit-based. A nurturing organization will be one where the focus is on hiring the right people and then training and developing them. The skills and abilities might not be apparent upfront, but people are helped into them."

At Fresh Tilled Soil, we chose the latter direction. Although we experimented with both types of people, we quickly learned that we were better at growing people than we were at hiring industry experts. The significance of our name and the idea of helping people grow was not lost on us. Culture is a living, breathing thing and that means you have to feed it to help it grow. The best way to feed your culture is to create ways for members of the team to bond with each other. The opportunities for bonding don't need to be cheesy or complicated. Simple is better. We particularly like this suggestion from BancVue's Skottie O'Mahony: "I did a presentation just about me that explained my background, explained how I got where I got, where my inspiration comes from, stuff like that." This presentation gave the team a chance to get to know Skottie and develop a deeper understanding of his viewpoints. "And I'm actually asking each team member to do the same thing, to share with the rest of the team, what their background is, what makes them tick, because I think that's really important for the rest of the people on the team and it will help the team."

Of course, people are way more complex than their resumes. Backgrounds and skills can't guarantee outcomes. When these leaders organize their businesses, they are doing so with outcomes in mind. "We recently did a reorganization of the company. Traditionally, we had been organized around departments," explains Tiffany Farriss about her Chicago-based design and development firm. "The departments were basically by discipline, so you might have the front-end developers. You might have your engineers. You might have designers. You might have your project managers. You'd have … silos, and the project teams were cut orthogonally against those." The reality of creating successful outcomes in design projects means the team isn't going to be organized by skills. "Your project teams could change based on the needs of the project. Who you were working with can change in any given time, and you work with them for the duration of that project. In some cases, you move on to the next project and you might have a whole new group of people to work with. What we've recently done is realized we want to enable these teams to really get to know each other and to start realizing the gains of being a … high-performing team. To do that, we created production units that are fully integrated. You have PMs, designers, devs, and engineers that will always work together, and a project will live within a single lane so we can deliver better results for our clients and then have the teams be more familiar, have that velocity gain that you have when you have a team that really does know how to work together."

ALIGNING PEOPLE WITH CULTURE

We've seen that a deliberate approach to culture provides a safe and creative place for people to do their best work. The question a lot of young leaders still ask is, "How do we get all these different people working together under a single cultural umbrella?" The answer to this question is nuanced. Our leaders often have wildly opposing views on how to do this. In our interviews and survey results, the vast majority of respondents agreed that culture was important, but not all agreed that directing it was possible.

We dug into these questions with our design leaders and asked them to tell us how they find the right people for their culture. "Am I looking for similar qualities? Yeah. Everybody fills a different role, so I'm not going to say if they don't laugh at my jokes, they're out the door," laughs Jeff Kushmerek, previously Chief Product Officer at FlashNotes and now VP of Professional Services at Virgin Pulse, who admits that a quirky sense of humor is something he's looking for in new hires. "We're with each other more than we're with our families, unfortunately. So, you do have to work with people that you're going to enjoy working with. Not everybody's got to be knee-slapping funny, but they can't be on the opposite end of that. 'That person's a jerk but man they can design their way out of a paper bag,' is not going to work out for you, you know?"

Diversity in personalities and skills might be the common thread in successful businesses, but not at the expense of personalities that want to keep learning. A learning culture suggests a maturity that will lead to problem-solving and growth. "Everyone can do a better job, no matter who they are. People that want to be better are easier to work with," says John Torres of America's Test Kitchen, creator of Cook's Illustrated. He reinforces the personal maturity aspects of this interaction. "I want to work with adults with personalities that mesh well together. I want to be solving problems with people who care about the outcomes and the people they worked with."

Tiffany Farriss warns that culture requires hard work and lots of communication. "The culture of trust really hinges on your ability to communicate with each other. A lot of that communication is around feedback. Making sure that anything that needs to be talked about gets talked about. Making sure that each person has the tools to talk about it appropriately and talk about it in a way that leads to a productive resolution." These communication loops aren't just going to impact individuals and direct relationships. "A culture of good communication helps with your projects. It helps with your team dynamic. It definitely helps your client. It's also a tremendous amount of work and takes a lot of effort."

The fact that culture requires a serious amount of attention and work is probably why so many companies fail at achieving a positive culture. The design leaders that impressed us the most were the leaders that invested a healthy amount of time in understanding culture and nurturing their company's culture. They didn't always know exactly what their culture would evolve to become, but they were deeply invested in guiding the culture as it evolved. These leaders reminded us of good parents, not obsessive helicopter parents.

Building a consensus around the culture is another tactic deployed by our leaders. Having the team agree on elements of culture allows them to buy into the outcome. By being included in the decision-making that leads to guidelines or policy, the team is also invested in the outcomes. This means increasing communication. When you increase opportunities for communication, you also increase understanding. "In today's context, it's very important in my opinion to, artificially at first, make different team members around the world have more video conversations than email or chat," says Karim Marucci of Crowd Favorite. "There's something that's lost in today's culture with only electronic communication, and that's the human aspect of just trying to make sure that we understand each other and what's important to each other. So it's been very difficult, yet very rewarding to try and figure that out with Skype video or Google Hangouts, or the new tools that are coming out. My company was one of the first companies that bought the Cisco system, back in the day, that cost over a hundred-thousand dollars, and now you can do it with eighty-dollar webcams. So it's about making sure that you set it up so people, even if they're not necessarily in the same room, can still feel part of the same team."

Thinking ahead to when his company is larger, Anthony Armendariz tells us, "The long-term goal for us, in terms of retention and not losing strong talent, is to get them where they need to be financially with competitive salaries. We offer a lot of benefits, but I still think we want to be able to bridge that gap and we also want to grow these people into leaders themselves. Obviously I love running this business, but I'm looking forward to the day when I don't necessarily have to be in every meeting or every call or every design review."

This last point is an important one. Allowing culture to support activities like talent acquisition is critical to sustained growth but it can't always be the responsibility of the leadership. As the company grows, the culture must mature enough to stand on its own feet. A design leader can't be at every touchpoint or fix the culture every time it falters. The design leader's best investment is to get everyone in the company to own the culture.

THE STRUCTURE OF CULTURE

How your team is structured will also influence the culture of your organization. Architecting culture can often be as simple as having certain people or roles sit next to each other. The more thoughtful the team structure, the bigger the impact. "We are entirely team-based," says Geoff Wilson. "Our entire organization is split into teams and we operate each team separately. A typical team for us consists of a project manager, a visual designer, a front-end developer, two software developers or back-end developers, depending on what you want to call them, and then a quality assurance tester. We also have user-experience professionals, UX researchers, and marketing strategists who can create copy and marketing strategy, so we will insert them into teams as well, depending on the needs of the particular project."

Wilson elaborates on how the teams work with clients and how this ultimately influences the culture of their firm. "If it's a consumer-facing project, you're almost assuredly going to have involvement from both UX and marketing on a project team, so the team will become a little bit bigger." The team is at the center of a series of concentric circles. These teams generate work that then generates a reputation for the company. This team-first organizational structure influences the culture of the company. "Our entire culture is centered around empowering our teams. We encourage our teams to name themselves [and] create their own set of values so that the team's values are compatible with the company's values, but we [also] encourage each team to have their own values set, their own way of working together, their own code of being, a code of conduct for members of their team. We really encourage our teams to take ownership, to own their client relationships, to act as their own small business unit within our agency. We give each of our teams a monthly morale budget, typically $250 per month per team, which the team uses to go out to dinner together, to go out for happy hour together, to go to a baseball game together, whatever the team chooses to do with it. But we encourage our teams to do something with that budget every month so they're constantly having an opportunity to continue to grow their personal relationships and celebrate their wins. As they achieve milestones in their projects, we want them to go out and be able to enjoy that outside of work together."

FINAL WORDS

Whether you believe culture can be created or merely guided, the consensus is unanimous—culture is critically important to company success. The people you hire have the biggest impact on your culture. Knowing this and taking the time to invest in the right hires results in a better business. Design leaders often point to the fact that although their jobs revolve around the design and development, their work is to bring the best team together. America's Test Kitchen's John Torres says it best. "Ultimately, as design leaders, we're building teams and companies, not products and things."

KEY TAKEAWAYS

- Culture is definitely a high priority for successfully run design businesses.

- To create culture, leaders need to construct the container and fill it with the right people. The container is made of the vision and values of the organization.

- Healthy cultures can be thought of as learning cultures, which have a growth mentality and a desire to challenge themselves.

- You can't create culture with ping-pong tables and beanbags.

- The people in your organization have the biggest influence on the culture.

- Even though you can't control every aspect of the culture, don't ignore it.

- Healthy culture appears to increase staff retention and loyalty.

- Team structures influence company culture. Select and combine team-mates carefully.

- Teams with mature attitudes toward personal growth are more likely to create a healthy culture.

- Growing successful teams and people is the ultimate goal of the design leader.

Talent

Introduction

In the early stages of a design company, finding the right talent to grow your team can seem like a distant problem. Particularly as you start out as a small group of founding members, seeking and developing talent on a regular basis simply isn't at the top of your mind. But for larger teams and established studios, it is something that needs to be addressed almost daily. As the company grows, even the most loyal team members move on and need replacing. Our design leaders are constantly having to ask how they will find and keep the best people.

The reasons people leave design firms vary. Some may leave due to a change in personal circumstances like getting married, having children, health concerns, or moving to a different state or country. Professional reasons for leaving a company are often characterized by the desire to move up or out. "Up" refers to ambition, whereas "out" is more likely due to dissatisfaction with the company or the leadership.

In our conversations, we learned that a significant reason people left teams was bad working relationships. What's noticeable is that these failing relationships were almost always with their managers—so it is not the company they are leaving but the manager relationship. The chemistry between team members and leaders seems to be the most often quoted reason for frustration. It may take a long time for these frustrations to result in an employee leaving, but once it reaches that point it is very difficult to persuade him or her to stay with the team.

In an industry that is increasingly competitive, retaining talent has become a top priority for the design leaders we interviewed. Something that makes design leadership even more challenging is the fact that larger, more resource-rich companies are eager to add design talent to their teams. A rash of acquisitions and design team creations by companies such as Capital One, IBM, Accenture, and

Deloitte is an indication that these larger companies intend on being part of the design landscape. Headhunting and poaching are an unfortunate reality of the design and technology world and this, combined with design schools and institutions struggling to keep up with demand, means design leaders face an uphill battle.

Fortunately, some design leaders have been successful in attracting and, more importantly, retaining top-notch talent. This chapter sheds some light on their best practices and inside secrets.

Small Teams and Building Out

Our interviews made it clear that for smaller companies or early-stage teams, an organic approach to growth is almost inevitable. In these startup stages, these small teams are mostly focused on getting the work done and are less concerned with a formal talent acquisition strategy, largely due to the fact that they almost always know the people they hire. Friends, family, and acquaintances are the pool from which new talent emerges for these fledgling businesses. Twenty percent of leaders interviewed told us that they relied on friends and family referrals for new hires.

As these companies grow, the hiring practices become, by necessity, more deliberate and structured. Very often these small teams don't have the luxury of support staff, and rely on a more formalized approach to help with the hiring process. In parallel with the changes of a growing team is the need to change focus from one type of skillset to another.

"When we went from 7 to 15 people, the focus for hiring was always on billable production people: developers and designers," says Dominic Bortolussi, founder of The Working Group in Toronto. "I was doing project management and Andres (Bortolussi's partner) was doing project management. So every single person in the company, until we were 15, or even up to 20, was pretty much a production person." In many of the companies we spoke to, this was the norm. Early employees would wear lots of different hats, which in essence was how they filled the gaps that would be filled by support staff further down the path of the business. As the teams got bigger, the requirement for more support staff was an organic and natural progression. Instead of being surprised by this change in hiring focus, mature leaders prepared for the transition.

Anthony Armendariz, who runs Funsize, a small but growing 11-person product design studio in Austin, relies on existing relationships for now. "In terms of the recruiting, it's all been organic. Today, we hired only people that we know personally or that someone we work with knows personally, or that we've had pretty good experience with. It's all referral-based recruiting, or we see someone we really want to work with and we'll try to find a way to work with them." Growing doesn't mean you can't hire your friends and family, but unless you have a large network, it might begin to get strained.

The hire-your-friends approach was reiterated by Marty Haught, founder of Boulder-based Haught Codeworks. "For many years, the people on the team were friends of mine that I've worked with over the years. I thought, 'I really liked working with him, and I want him to work with me on these projects.' So a lot of it was that." Haught acknowledges that as they've grown, this strategy is giving way to an approach that includes some formal onboarding and training. "But lately, I've brought on two more junior members. One is actually doing a formal apprenticeship with Haught Codeworks. They've come recommended by some friends of mine." When it comes to talent, the importance of your network is a constant theme for these design leaders.

From our conversations, it seems that startups and smaller design firms rely on their personal networks for talent. This makes perfect sense until the company grows to a point where these structures need to be formalized, unless the company is receiving outside funding and plans on growing quickly. We encountered only a handful of independently owned design companies that intend on quick growth with the help of external funding. Venture-funded service design startups are extremely rare and were not part of the scope of our interviews.

Developing Talent Is Similar to Developing a Sales Pipeline

Approaching the talent pipeline in the same way that successful companies approach sales seems to be the key to finding great people. For service and product companies alike, to achieve sustained growth without pain, you need a solid list of potential hires in your pipeline. If the sales pipeline is the lifeblood of a service business, then the talent pipeline is the air it breathes. For design teams that work within larger organizations, the talent pipeline might be their core strategic effort. Acknowledging that talent development is an ongoing effort that requires patience and planning is a trait we recognized in the most successful design leaders.

Carl White of Think Brownstone is emphatic about this. "We treat recruiting like we do business development. It's about relationships and it's going to take time. Our pipeline for candidates is as active as our new business pipeline. We spend a lot of time, sometimes up to three months, recruiting folks. If we find someone that stands out, we have a conversation with them, likely in-person."

Even with the knowledge that establishing a talent pipeline is critical, many leaders are still not sure where to start. The key appears to lie in having a public conversation about the company and the work. "Being good about sharing everything that we know," says Brian Williams, CEO of Viget. "We've been blogging for years. We try to go to conferences and speak at conferences as much as we can. We encourage the staff to do that. We try to host events when we can in our space, to see what's suitable and helpful for folks. So just being a good member of the community is an important part of that, but really just trying to build up the reputation: do great work, share the work, be able to talk about that, and do the little things that help people understand what the culture is all about. That tends to create a lot of connections and a lot of people come in that way."

Throwing a wide net creates a funnel that attracts talent to you, which means there are always prospects knocking at the door. Turning people away is a better problem to have than wondering where your next hire is coming from.

Just like in sales pipelines, there will be some opportunities that take longer to close than others. Occasionally, an ideal candidate may come along but they already have a great job or the timing to join you isn't quite right yet. This is part of the process, explains White. "If it's a good fit and it's a match, then we keep them moving along, but there are a lot of times we don't have an opportunity for them yet. I bet a third of the time, that's the way it's happened: 'I like you, you like me, but I'm in a relationship right now. If I get out of it, and when the stars align, let's get together.' That's worked really, really well for us."

Like a sales pipeline, flexibility is required and not all hiring strategies need to be the same. "If you're looking for a more senior hire, there's a certain point in their career when they are simply never going to get hired via a job board or requisition again," Jennifer Dary, head of the consultancy Plucky reminds us. "They'll get hired over drinks or lunch where you'll have several strategic conversations discussing your needs and theirs. It's so important to remember that these more senior hires will arrive in your pipeline differently than, say, a junior person fresh out of school. Your pipeline has to be flexible enough to account for a variety of paths and introductions."

Understanding how each team hires and grows requires an understanding of the type of culture a company supports. In the case of nGen Works, "The team actually hired the team," says Carl Smith. He adds, "One of the things I'm really happiest about is that we realized early on, if you want people to have a sense of loyalty, you have to make sure that the people they're working with are the people who wanted them. The core team actually seeks out people they want to work with and invites them in to work on a project. That's the onboarding process. You actually join the team that wanted you on a project. Over time, if it works out, they hire you. The team hires the team."

There is a key point to make here: team members are not adding people to the team at random; instead, once a project has been approved by the client, the team members invite freelancers with specific project-related skills to join them on those projects. If a freelancer consistently provides value to the team, then they may be invited to join the company full-time. "Now the flipside is when the team fires the team. It's very much like Survivor. If it gets to a point where you're just not doing well, you will get voted off the island," cautions Smith. "They've jokingly started referring to me being voted off the island. I'm fine with it," he laughs. Although I like many aspects of this approach, I'm personally not comfortable with letting the team make the final decision on new hires. Very often, a leader needs to add people that might not be the popular choice but are required to move the team forward. I love the idea of having the team involved in the decision to hire new team members but ultimately believe the leader's job is to make the final choice.

Actively creating opportunities to meet new talent was a theme that came up again and again in our conversations. With only a few exceptions, all of the interviewed leaders had a specific strategy to add new candidates to their talent funnel. Although hiring strategies varied widely, the consistent feature was that they weren't left to chance; there was always a planned approach, with senior leadership involvement every step of the way.

"We've actually been talking about that over the last couple of days," Alex King, Crowd Favorite's founder and CEO at the time of the interview pointed out. "One of the things I've done is write a document about how I've gone through the vetting process of candidates to try to share with the people that are going to be sharing that responsibility going forward." At our meeting in early 2014, King's company had recently been acquired when, because of health concerns, King had begun to shift some of the responsibilities[1] from himself to other hiring managers. "We also have talked a little bit more about tailoring our job postings,

---

1 Alex King tragically passed away in late September 2015. After our interview, he left Crowd Favorite so he could focus on managing his health and spending time with his family. The digital design industry lost a great leader and friend.

making them more specific to the types of responsibilities and goals people will have in those roles in order to try to help people self-select out if it's not a good fit for what they want ... to make hiring more of an ongoing process, rather than something that we do just whenever there's a need."

WHICH CAME FIRST, THE SKILLS OR THE PASSION?

Recruiting, interviewing, and onboarding new team members is arguably the company leader's highest priority. Our leaders all agreed that having the right people has such far-reaching effects that knowing how to get them on your team is critical. What's not so clear is whether leaders should be hunting for great skills or seeking out passionate people who can learn them.

"I'm a big fan of the scenario-based interview," says Dave Gray, President of XPLANE. "So what you really want to know when you're interviewing someone is how they operate in difficult situations or how they handle interpersonal issues. I might ask them questions like: 'Tell me about a time where you had an interpersonal conflict at work and what you did about it. Tell me about a time when you failed at something and learned a really important lesson that you still carry with you today. Tell me about the best boss you ever had. Tell me about the worst boss you ever had. Worst coworker, best project, things like that. And what I'm looking for in a situational interview is, how does this person operate? How do they see the social systems that they're in? How do they handle conflict? I think that's very important. Do they avoid it? Do they address it? In what way do they interact with other people to get work done? Describe the kind of situation you think they'll find themselves in at work and see if you can identify and get from them similar situations they've been in in the past and how they thought about it, how they handled it."

Finding the right chemistry also means setting your sights on the right qualities. "You don't find good talent—you find great people and you develop talent," says Zurb founder and CEO Bryan Zmijewski. "If you think you're going to find a rock star, good luck." This idea that talent is crafted—and not something people are born with—came up regularly in our interviews. Design leaders acknowledge that people may come with a passion for design but that the talent for good design can be taught. "I've never been of the mindset that there's a perfect employee, a perfect person," continues Zmijewski. "You kind of adapt your organization to people who are very passionate about what they're doing, who have a good work ethic and respect each other. When you foster an environment like that, you'd be amazed at how much potential comes out of people."

Hire People Smarter than You

It may be a little cliché, but it's a mantra we heard frequently: hire people who are smarter than you are. Interestingly, these design leaders are not just hiring smart people, they are hiring smart people who can carry forward the vision of the company in ways the founders may not be able to. "I hire people that are much better than I could ever be at what they do," says Tracey Halvorsen, President and Chief Visionary Officer at Baltimore-based FastSpot. "I have great designers, great programmers, great project managers. I always think that what I'm best at is helping get everyone to move along, but they're much better at doing the stuff. They make me look good."

It's not just finding people who are smart but also people who are committed to their organization's goals and to their craft. As Bortolussi at The Working Group points out, "The objective then is to find people who are aligned with how we work. We enjoy our work together, we ask for excellence, and we have a lot of fun doing it. So we look for people who are aligned with that and who are really good at what they do and want a career as a master craftsman—whether that's as a developer or designer."

Hiring people who are smarter than you isn't enough. You also have to hire people who are different than you. Diversity isn't just an intellectual challenge—it's the secret sauce of successful design firms.

DIVERSITY OF SKILLS

Closely related to the idea of hiring people with superior soft and hard skills is the idea that not all skilled people should be considered equal. Hard skills are generally technical skills like programming, using a design application, or proposal writing. Soft skills refer to things like communication, presentation, and conflict resolution. These latter skills can sometimes be harder to assess, but they are the skills that successful design companies rely on to deliver real value to their clients. Some hires are going to make terrific individual contributions while others will take on broader management roles. Understanding whose strengths and weaknesses fit into the jigsaw puzzle of a company's organization is key to a team's success.

We asked our design leaders what they are always looking for in terms of team skills and chemistry. Jeb Banner, CEO and cofounder of Smallbox, located in Indianapolis, likes people who push him out of his comfort zone. "I want people who are unafraid to challenge me and others but have the skills to do it in a loving, kind way. I want people who are better than me. In a way, the fact that

I'm not a designer and developer hurts sometimes, because I have trouble being a collaborator on those things where I'd like to be. But I really look for people who have talents and skills that I just look at and say, 'Wow. I can't imagine having this skillset' because every time I see something they do, it makes me think in a wider way about the potential. So I always want people to broaden my thinking, not narrow it."

Building teams around the idea of "who's on the bus" and who still needs to get on the bus came up several times during our interviews. The bus metaphor, originally developed by the business researcher and author Jim Collins,[2] appeared in the business classic *Good to Great*. Throughout the interviews, the idea was regularly referred to directly or in concept and appears to resonate with the approach that many of the leaders we met with have employed. Collin's idea suggests that each company is like a bus about to head off for a destination—metaphorically, its mission or purpose. Putting the right people on the bus, seated in the right seats, and getting the wrong people off the bus, is one of the lessons from Collins' book. "I think the biggest thing I look for when I'm hiring new members is what's missing from the team," says Skottie O'Mahony, Creative Director for BancVue. "I look for someone who has some talent or some background or some experience that the other people on the team can learn from."

Critical to success in the design space is finding people with both hard and soft skills. So much of the design process is people-orientated that those working at high-performing design firms and interfacing with clients require excellent writing and presentation skills. O'Mahony says, "Now that we have dedicated project managers, it's an interesting skillset: we want detail-oriented people who enjoy the communication, people who are able to manage clients, manage the accounts well. It's a different skillset than what a developer needs to have." Building teams of people with different skillsets raises the tide for the whole group. Diversity in skills, backgrounds, and thinking appears to encourage everyone on the team to be more empathetic and understanding—a critical part of all design disciplines.

O'Mahony, whose product design team numbered 30 when we interviewed him, has the same holistic view of diversity that we encountered among the majority of the design leaders. "I was looking for people that had user research

---

2 Jim Collins *Good to Great: Why Some Companies Make the Leap... And Others Don't* (New York: Harper Collins, 2001).

experience because we didn't have that on the team. People that had different backgrounds—like illustration or video—because it's those areas that we would like to grow in, but are still in their infancy. I figured if I could get people on the team that had that experience, they would help the entire team."

Gender is the diversity elephant in the room. There is definitely a gender bias toward more male designers in our industry. Several leaders we spoke to were concerned about this. "We've got a very diverse team here, but we're trying to get it more gender-balanced as well, which is another challenge," admits The Working Group's Dominic Bortolussi. "We're sort of becoming the classic agency, where half the designers are women and all the developers are men. We're trying to change that, and we're trying to encourage that change is ongoing." This problem isn't just about equal opportunity; gender diversity brings the necessary diversity of perspective so critical for good design. Many initiatives to balance the gender inequity are being undertaken. This topic is important but too broad for the parameters of this book. We hope to see the design industry create a good example for all other industries.

Grow out of Your Shoes, Not into Them

Talent growth can be structured and planned, but this does not mean you have to hire ahead of your immediate needs. Anthony Armendariz shared his anxieties about hiring with us at the Funsize office overlooking bustling 6th Street in Austin. "We assembled the team by being scared. Natalie (Funsize cofounder) and I were really worried about payroll. We had never been put in a situation where we had to pay payroll, and so in the early days we were kind of scared. Everyone has always started out as a contractor, so we made sure they fit in culturally, had the contributions we needed, the right skills. Then it usually resulted in a relationship that we didn't want to lose, so we began growing that way. Once we realized we had five or six people, it became pretty clear that we needed to make long-term, full-time hire commitments."

It's worth reiterating that formalizing hiring is not the same as getting ahead of company growth. Talent is a design services firm's highest cost. Adding team members has to be done with care but not so slowly that it hurts productivity. This balancing act isn't easy. Our leaders repeatedly mentioned that this dance between adding new talent and getting the best out of their existing team was a constant struggle. The most successful leaders used their sales pipeline to dictate their staffing needs.

Letting the future growth needs of the company dictate hiring decisions might seem like the straightforward approach. Logic suggests that you should plan ahead for hiring and stick to that plan. In the world of design services, that's not always the best way forward. Planning too far ahead can defy the reality of the situation. If you don't have the client work to pay for the growth in staff, hiring based on a plan alone can backfire.

To punctuate this lesson is a cautionary tale from Greg Hoy, the CEO of Happy Cog: "Some of the staffing decisions that we've made were probably a bit ambitious in terms of getting a number of people in at one time to satisfy a need that we anticipated. Staffing up to support a pipeline that looks one way one week and another way two weeks later is a roll of the dice. Hopefully, you have put enough thought behind it so it's not going to be a situation where you have too many people." In early 2014, Happy Cog started experimenting with a "team-based model" and preemptively hired designers and developers to fill one of their teams. When business development expectations changed and they were unable to service this team, they had to make the tough decision to let the some of those people go. Greg remains philosophical about those lessons and reminds us that it's always the sales pipeline that determines your growth.

Ultimately, the design leaders we spoke to agreed that they would rather have a slightly understaffed team than carry the overhead of underutilized people. Although it can be daunting to take on work when you don't have the people to deliver it, it's easier to fill in the gaps than to deal with the stressful burden of a negative cash flow. This is generally true of small- to medium-sized service agencies, but may not be true of well-funded startups, larger companies, or internal design teams. The latter group will often have a longer runway of cash or alternative sources of income to support team growth in anticipation of required work.

It's not always about hiring the right people at the wrong time, and then finding the company overstaffed without the workflow to support these new hires. There's danger, too, in hiring the wrong people for the wrong reasons. Each hire should contribute to the needs of the overall team and fill any skill gaps within that team. "You should never be in a massive rush to hire the wrong person," says Jeff Kushmerek, currently head of product at Virgin Pulse. "That person who's dying for a job because he's got mouths to feed, you should never jump into the wrong thing, because he's going to be unhappy with me, or my style, or unhappy with the job that's put in front of him as well." Kushmerek goes on to say that he's looking for complementary skills as well. "We should always fill in those holes. You don't want people who are just going to be a replica of yourself."

This sentiment was almost universal in our interviews. When hiring, successful design leaders look for people with common values but who also have skills that fill the gaps in their current teams. You might say that the ideal candidate for these design leaders will have similar goals, values, and communication styles but different experiences, perspectives, and skills.

Hire Coachable People Willing to Learn

Many of the successful leaders we interviewed preferred hiring younger talent and then investing time and money in teaching them the skills they need. This wasn't a majority opinion, but it certainly was the most popular approach. Specifically, they would hire younger talent who displayed good soft skills or showed potential. In the design industries, soft skills refer to communication and people skills. Being a good presenter or communicator or having conflict resolution skills appealed to our leaders far more than the ability to push pixels or write code. Thirty-seven percent of leaders interviewed said that they preferred to "hire young and train them up."

One important consideration with this approach is that youth cannot be a substitute for maturity and experience. There are certainly mature young designers and developers out there, but it's unlikely that every young candidate will have the level of maturity or depth of experience you seek. Furthermore, youth often comes with the requirement of training in new skills. If you're not set up to train relatively inexperienced staff, this approach can slow productivity down. This was something we experienced first-hand at Fresh Tilled Soil and it was reaffirmed by Jon Lax, cofounder of Teehan+Lax. "We learned very early on that we weren't that great at hiring junior staff and coaching them up. We were just better off when people had a little bit more maturity. As a result, we tend to hire people who are maybe in their third or fourth year of their career before they come here."

As we discussed in the chapter on culture, the type of organization you create will either support hiring practices aimed at attracting highly polished expertise or developing young rough diamonds. Hiring younger designers, developers, or project managers may appear to be a cost-saving strategy but comes with the clear disadvantage that those people won't always have the experience you need. This requires an investment of time to develop the missing skills and may cancel out some of the benefits of cheaper talent.

Plucky's Jennifer Dary warns against the tendency to think of junior talent as a cost-saving strategy. "I completely agree that homegrown talent can be some of the most loyal and culturally dynamic members of a team. But I also want to point out that many agencies will hire junior folks to save some money without building the infrastructure to mentor these people. It's sink or swim. The millennial generation in particular prefers mentorship and explicit guidance. I see it time and time again: organizations hire junior and assign them to the busiest person at the place. Mentoring takes time, effort, and bandwidth. You may be saving money on salary, but you've got to be ready to spend a senior person's hours to invest in the hire as well." Dary's caution is something we heard repeated by our design leaders. Although most agreed that despite there being a real cost to training and mentoring, the investment is well worth it. Design leaders thinking that young, cheap talent is a shortcut might ultimately pay the price further down the line.

Hiring senior designers and developers brings its own set of challenges: cost being the most obvious and, in some cases, bad habits learned elsewhere. Many of the leaders interviewed for this book expressed concern about hiring before getting to know the candidate. This underlines the preference successful design leaders have for soft skills and good chemistry. Just having hard skills very often is not enough in such a collaborative industry. A good proportion of them recommend the "try before you buy" approach, described by Carl White, CEO and founder of Philadelphia-based design studio Think Brownstone. "Some of the brightest people we've hired haven't had a lot of experience in this field, but they're some of our best folks. We can tell, once you meet folks and they do some 'ride alongs' with us, you can see them grabbing on to it and doing it. They've been our best." This approach is also catching on in more formal apprenticeship-based models. The successful nature of design apprenticeships has been long known in Europe and Japan but is only recently starting to catch on in North America. More on this topic at the end of the chapter.

Connected to hiring coachable people is hiring talent with the motivation to succeed. "I don't know if I'm going to get in trouble for saying this, but I love hiring immigrants, first-generation people," says Bortolussi. "They've got all the passion—building a career in a new country and a new place. Their work ethic is amazing, attitude is amazing, there's no self-entitlement. This is, of course, not to say that everyone who isn't a first generation or an immigrant doesn't have that. I don't go out of my way to hire immigrants, but I find that we have a high number of people who have recently settled in Canada, or whose parents are settled in Canada. I don't know why that is, but we all get along really well. I think maybe it's the nature of the industry. It's STEM-focused, there's a lot of science, the technology piece of it tends to favor a lot of people from Asia, Southeast Asia, as well as the Middle East." As an immigrant myself, I support Bortolussi's insights. Coming to the US from another country means you have a lot at stake. Your family's expectations, proving your worth, and not wanting to let your own culture down are just a few of the considerations an immigrant might face. These externalities can be powerful motivators.

John Torres, Digital Design Director of America's Test Kitchen, agrees with finding the right motivations. "I'm looking for small egos. Smart people who are passionate about the outcome, rather than about putting their stamp on the thing."

At Fresh Tilled Soil, we took the idea that the best talent is coachable, and created the Apprentice in User Experience, or AUX. In an effort to stay on top of our talent needs we developed a 110-day program that also includes a pre-program boot camp to sift out the pretenders. The goal is to turn promising designers and developers into UX pros through structured learning, one-on-one mentorship, and client-facing experience. Apprentices that make it through boot camp are paired with a mentor to help guide them through the challenges. All apprentices participate in lectures and several challenges meant to develop new skills. They also get to work on client projects for valuable real-world experience. Once they graduate, they either join our team as full-time employees or are placed with partner or client teams. These apprenticeship programs are becoming increasingly popular in the design space. Established programs are available at industry leadership companies like Sparkbox, Thoughtbot, Upstatement, Merge, and Detroit Labs. Given the success of these programs, more will no doubt follow.

Growing Teams

Reflecting on Jim Collin's bus metaphor again, leaders will need to know who stays on the bus, who gets off, and what new seats need to be filled. The threat is that hiring managers don't simply hire people who are just like them. Scott Baldwin, Director of User Experience Design at Yellow Pencil's Vancouver office, reminds us that hiring "clones" isn't going to satisfy the needs of the organization. "I find, in a lot of cases, that doesn't create an interesting tension within the group. If you have people of mixed cultures, if that makes sense, or mixed personalities, I think you get a more interesting and dynamic team."

As companies grow, so does the complexity of the hiring process. Firms and teams that once relied on word-of-mouth talent referrals are now faced with new problems: job diversification and pipeline volume. "Once we hit a certain point, somewhere after the twenties, it became painfully evident that we needed a few more types of roles built in there," says Dominic Bortolussi. Smaller companies require their people to wear multiple hats. As teams expand, this becomes unsustainable. With the segmentation of jobs comes the necessity to hire more deliberately for those specific roles. "More project management, more product management, an office coordinator, an office admin. Now we have an HR person. There's a number of roles that emerged over time, and so that's how the team has shifted. So now when I'm interviewing people," says Bortolussi, "I'm still looking for that lifestyle and cultural fit, so that we know people will get along, but the skillset is broadened from being just an amazing designer or helper, to having a lot of other types of skills."

Think Brownstone's White, who prefers to work with candidates as freelancers before committing to full-time roles, admits, "As we've gotten bigger and our process is a little more fleshed out, we probably do less of the try-before-you-buy approach. It's going to get harder, too. We have somebody right now that has no experience in this field but who we think would be great."

Diversity of experience means diversity of opinion and an increasing need for good chemistry within the team. As teams grow, it's naive to think that everyone you hire will have the perfect set of skills or consistently agree on the approach to the problems you're solving. The key is to find good chemistry between the team members. A well-bonded team can work well together even if they have differing opinions about the work. As discussed throughout this chapter, ensuring diversity in growing teams is key to our leader's success. "I hired people who have opinions about everything. So even if you're a UI designer, you should have an opinion about UX," says John Torres. "I want to work with adults with personalities that mesh well together. It's my job to build teams and companies, not products and things." This last point by John might be the best thing we've heard about design leadership: the leader's job is not to create the designs but to create the team and culture to give birth to these designs. This is the ultimate role for leaders in the acquisition or creation of talent.

Finding personalities that gel well together while allowing for robust debate when necessary gives teams the variety of perspectives so crucial in great design work. This isn't always straightforward when a team is already established. When old habits and dominant personalities are well established, there is a different set of challenges facing leaders. In many cases, the grooves have been well worn and changing them is extremely hard. Over time, and without even realizing it, teams can start to look too homogeneous. "There are managers who essentially hire themselves, and there are managers who hire different people," observes Yellow Pencil's Baldwin, "and I look for a mix of both. People that diversify and play off skillsets that I don't have, or where I can learn something from them as much as they're learning from me. Ideally, we should be working collectively as a team, and growing in that way. Whereas I think in a lot of cases, managers will hire replicas of themselves."

When we met with Neil McPhedran, General Manager at Grey in Vancouver, he had recently taken on the general manager role. He was inheriting an existing team but had the opportunity to reorganize it. We asked him about how he approached these challenges from both a team-creation and an ongoing cultural point of view. "When I walked in the door, there had been a few moves made with some folks who had been here for a long time, so we had a good core that was still here. It's taken some time to assess opinions from other folks as to who should be and who shouldn't be here and I've definitely come at it from a different perspective. I've got a different take on things since I'm on ground here and can feel it versus what management in Toronto thought."

Talented people come from many walks of life. Differences in personalities and cultures breathes new ideas into a design conversation. The path they've taken to becoming designers or developers is just as varied as the personalities. Traditional design education isn't the only way to get to the design industry. "I think I've come across two paths," says Greg Storey, whose career includes being founder of Airbag Industries and CMO of Happy Cog. "I've hired and worked with students who came out of design school where they have a lot of tactical experience. They kind of paraded through applications and a little bit of history, a little bit of process, more of the how-to stuff. And then, I've come across and worked with a lot of people who just taught themselves everything they needed to know along the way and felt more street-smart. There's definitely a place for both."

FINDING BALANCE AND LETTING GO

The flipside of any talent acquisition strategy is knowing when to disinvest. John Torres, Digital Design Director at America's Test Kitchen, says, "If you're having a lot of meetings to talk about a particular ongoing behavior or what someone is doing wrong or how they react to others, then you are spending too much time on that person, and they need to go." We like this perspective on letting people go and it might be distilled into a question that design leaders can ask them-selves: "If I had to hire this person all over again, would I?" The answer to that question should give leaders a clear path to the decision to either break ties or invest more into that team member.

Part of considering whether someone should stay or go can be gleaned from taking their perspective on the situation. Very often, someone who you might feel is questionable is feeling the same way. They might already be thinking about moving on and they just need to have that conversation. "It might be in recogniz-ing that certain people on that team just really aren't meant to be part of that team, or that group, or that job function," says Scott Baldwin of Yellow Pencil. "I've had a few people in my career who clearly weren't passionate about the work that they were doing, and just didn't belong there. They're kind of along for the ride." Part of discovering their perspective, he goes on to say, "was encourag-ing them to find the kind of thing that they were passionate about. Realizing that it wasn't here, and allowing them to figure out their own exit, versus giving them the kick out the door." This approach benefits both sides. It's less about what's wrong and more about finding what's right. Their performance, or lack thereof, might be the most obvious thing to talk about, but digging a bit will reveal a deeper opportunity for both the leader and the team member.

Letting people go isn't always about individual performance. If the company or team is struggling and under financial pressure, layoffs need to happen. Lay-ing off good people is one of the hardest things a leader will have to do. The les-son here is to build a team that balances the need for high productivity with what the organization can afford. Overinvesting in a team can force layoffs when the work pipeline dries up or the funding slows down. Hire only when you abso-lutely have to, as XPLANE's Dave Gray learned the hard way. "Hiring people and then having to let them go—that was a very painful thing. When you've had lay-offs in your company, it makes you a lot more conscious and conservative in terms of growth and hiring. That morning, I was coming in to work having to lay off about half the workforce and one guy that was going to get laid off told me that he had just bought a house. He walked in the door and was like 'I bought a house!' And I was like, 'Oh, man.' You don't want to have that feeling. You don't want to do that to people. So, my feeling, my lesson is: hire slowly."

The beneficial outcome of this hard-learned lesson is that XPLANE has since developed a policy that supports growth but doesn't subject the business to stress when inevitable fluctuations happen. Gray explains, "We have a policy at XPLANE to do about 20 to 30 percent of our work with contractors and freelancers, because we have that kind of fluctuation in our business. We don't want to be hiring people and letting them go and creating that kind of see-saw effect. We want to always maintain a certain balance of the work between full-time and part-time and freelance people that gives us a lot more consistency and slow and steady growth."

This was a hiring strategy used at several of the companies we interviewed, but be careful as this approach can be a legal quagmire. It's worth noting that, in most states, state and federal law prohibits companies from keeping on freelancers when the work they are doing is stated as a core service of the firm. For example, if your business offers web design services, you cannot employ a freelance web designer for any extended period of time. How do you know whether you're bumping up against the law with your freelancers? The golden rule is: if it looks like a duck, swims like a duck, and quacks like a duck, then it probably is a duck.

Apprenticeships

In Western Europe, apprenticeship programs have been around for a very long time and are integrated into the fabric of almost all industries. The apprenticeship model is new to the North American working culture but it seems to be catching on in the design space. Several design leaders mentioned apprenticeship programs as a high-value way to get the best talent into their organizations.

It's important to note that an apprenticeship is not an internship. The goal of most apprenticeships is to receive a very specific hands-on design education from the organization and eventually get promoted to a full-time designer, developer, or strategist. If recruited correctly, the apprenticeship position is held by someone who already has a formal education and some experience in the industry. Most apprentices are seeking roles above the entry-level positions normally serviced by internships and probationary contracts. Positions are limited and the bar is normally high for qualification into the program, so only a few applicants make it into these programs.

The small numbers of apprentices are made up for by the high quality of the graduates. Unlike internships where the intern is padding their resume or just exploring options for their career, the design apprenticeships are for those that have already committed to a career in design. Whereas internships might be unpaid and aimed at part-time employees who are still in school, the apprenticeships are almost always full-time paid positions for college graduates. The companies we interviewed that run apprenticeship programs have very specific full-time roles to fill. For the programs to have the deepest impact on the company, the apprentices work side-by-side with senior team members on actual client work.

Many design leaders also see apprenticeships as a smarter alternative to using recruiters. Outsourcing the acquisition of talent is not only expensive but risky too. On average, recruiters charge 20% of the first year's salary of the placed employee. Unfortunately, this is not the most expensive part of recruiting this way. The real cost will come when recruits aren't matched technically or culturally to the company. Poorly matched hires can result in longer-term problems like retraining, team conflicts, and—possibly the worst—having to lay the hire off and start the hiring process from scratch. When hires are done on the basis of resumes and interviews alone, design leaders are essentially placing a bet on them.

Bad chemistry between new and existing team members is one of the most frequently mentioned reasons projects run into problems. Apprenticeships reduce that risk by giving leaders several weeks, or months, to get to know the candidates and integrate them into their teams. Furthermore, these candidates are often on client-facing teams, giving leaders further insight into their soft skills in dealing with tough situations. If those weren't enough reasons to run an apprenticeship program, the design leaders we spoke to also considered apprenticeships to be profit centers. Unlike interns, which are junior and perform low-value work, apprentices almost always work on client projects and are therefore billable.

Let's take a closer look at how these programs work to achieve these outcomes. At Fresh Tilled Soil, we've been running a successful apprenticeship program for the last 3 years. The program is called AUX (Apprentice in User Experience) and works like this:

- We run three semesters per year.

- Three times a year, we announce through our channels that a session is accepting applications and we receive about 25–35 applicants.

- Applicants go through a round of phone interviews, reference checks, code audits, and portfolio reviews.

- From the initial group, about 10–12 are selected to participate in a two-week "design thinking" boot camp.

- The boot camp is held on two consecutive Saturdays (each lasting about 4–5 hours).
- Participants in the boot camp work on several challenges and the best candidates are selected for the full-time program.
- Only 4–5 candidates are selected from the boot camp.
- The program is 16 weeks of paid full-time employment.
- The AUX's time is divided into 50% training and 50% client work. In other words, they are 50% billable.
- At the end of the 15 weeks, we select the top AUX graduates and offer them full-time jobs. On average, two will get offers.
- Graduates that don't get offers for full-time positions at the firm will get introductions to other companies looking for designers.

The math:

- The selection process requires about 15–20 hours from a senior person to manage. That's about $3,750–$5,000 of the program manager's time in billable terms.
- Additionally, training and mentoring takes about 5 hours per week. This workload is split between the entire team of 30 designers, developers, strategists, and project managers.
- When combining these indirect expenses, each cohort costs about $18,000 to manage.
- Over the three semesters, the annualized cost is about $54,000.
- Apprentices are paid $500/week, so that works out to $8,000 per apprentice for the 16 weeks. That's about $96,000 per year.
- All in, we spend about $150K per year to get 12 exceptionally well-trained designers and developers.
- We bill approximately $300K–$350K for their total time over the year.
- Dollars paid to recruiters: $0.

- Net profit: $150K–$200K per year.

The benefits:

- We are in control of which candidates we invest our time and money in.
- We can train candidates in the areas that fit best with our client work.
- Observing their soft skills (communication, presentation, conflict resolution, etc.) in challenging team and client situations is invaluable.
- We can monitor for cultural fit or personality conflicts.
- It's profitable!
- Graduates that don't get full-time jobs at Fresh Tilled Soil are introduced to our clients, partners, and friends. There are now over 35 graduates working at various places around the US. Several of these placements have resulted in referral work.

Apprentice programs have some shortfalls. These programs need supervision from senior team members throughout the year. Design leaders without a senior team to rely on for this support may struggle to find time for these activities. Apprenticeships are also not ideal for recruiting senior or executive staff members. Our design leaders didn't feel this was necessarily a problem because realistically those high-level positions would come from either internal promotions or their own professional network.

For detailed information on apprenticeship programs in North America, visit *http://apprentice.at/*.

FINAL WORDS

Almost none of the companies we interviewed used external recruiters to find new talent. We found this surprising considering the high volume of calls and emails we receive from recruiters at our own firm. However, the majority of the companies we spoke to either have a strong reputation in the community—which, by default, will attract talent—or run internal programs to develop junior talent, and in these ways are consciously nurturing the talent pipeline we have discussed in this chapter. Our experience, both as practitioners of talent development and having never relied on recruiters ourselves, is that it is possible to grow your team without the help of external recruiters. The caveat to this is that a few of the larger companies we interviewed used an internal recruiter or human resources person to fill that void.

Jennifer Dary leaves us with some key questions to keep in mind about retaining talent. "Companies spend a lot of money hiring people. From the job postings, to the hours spent interviewing, to the referral fees, it really adds up. Hiring, frankly, is a boring and expensive problem to solve. What is *more* interesting to me is retention and the strategies we put together in this area. Why are you losing bright people? How would your culture need to evolve to keep them? How are you tackling career paths (or not)? These are vital questions that need to be answered in any retention strategy."

In our chapter on culture, we provided insight into these questions.

KEY TAKEAWAYS

- A talent pipeline is just like a sales pipeline—invest in it constantly.
- Hire people who are smarter than you.
- When possible, hire people with great soft skills and train the hard skills.
- Diversity adds to the creativity and wisdom of the team.
- Coachable people are often better than knowledgeable people.
- Hiring young or inexperienced people isn't always a cost saving.
- Hire when capacity is consistently at its maximum, but not before.
- Consider freelancers to buffer for the ups and downs of your business cycles.
- Apprenticeships are invaluable and an alternative to expensive recruiting models.
- Apprentice programs can be great talent pipelines and profit centers.

Office Space and Remote Working

Introduction

There is no doubt that our physical space and coworkers play a huge part in how we feel about our day-to-day work. In this chapter, our design leaders share their ideas and hacks on a range of working environments and structures. From the quality of the light, to team organization and the length of the commute, our leaders have invested a lot of time and money into these work and play spaces. We discovered a rich diversity of office spaces, policies, and structures that help teams stay connected, productive, and happy. There's definitely no one-size-fits-all approach, but finding the space that aligns with your team and culture can be a productivity multiplier.

One of the clear advantages that technology offers is the opportunity to work remotely. Recently, there has been a lot of discussion in the media about whether teams should be expected to work in the office or allowed to work from home. Even within the office space, there are widely differing views on whether office floor plans should be open or closed. Somewhere in between these are the teams that have an office but frequently skip the commute to work from home. We found a broad range of approaches and would be hard-pressed to claim that one system works better than any other. However, we did discover that well-connected and productive teams didn't leave organization and structure to chance. The most successful design and development teams have clear policies about how to work, both in the office space and when working remotely. The best outcomes are also supported by technology and tools to keep everyone feeling productive. Seventy-five percent of design leaders suggest that physical space is very important to encouraging creativity.

Office spaces can suggest how leaders perceive themselves, and parallel how they define their roles. While companies are growing, so too are their leaders. Personal growth often tracks the company's evolving needs for physical space. As teams grow and the leader's role changes, we can see a connection between the design leader's approach and the physical space around them. Tracey Halvorsen, CEO of FastSpot, describes this transition from early stage to established company. "I think when you're just a couple of people in the living room, you don't really see yourself as the leader. You see yourself—because you're in the trenches—with everyone else panicking and trying to pay the rent and find work and make things happen." Once the company reaches a size where work is more consistent and the daily panic is replaced with more strategic goals, the physical spaces need to reflect that maturity.

Selecting a Location

Where you choose to stick your flag in the ground can influence everything from culture to recruiting talent. From the choice of city to the decor of your building—everything matters. Access to your clients and talent pool will very often be the priority for design teams that need frequent face-to-face time with their clients and team members. For remote teams that don't need to collaborate face-to-face or share a whiteboard, physical space is confined to their home office or a coffee shop. This doesn't mean that remote spaces should be exempt from the culture of the organization. Suggestions on how to organize those remote locations can be critical to daily project success. Making sure high-speed connections are available and distractions are kept to a minimum will help both remote workers and their teammates back at the office.

One of the highlights of this book was traveling to the various offices around North America to conduct the interviews. We traveled from Boston to almost 20 cities to meet in person with the design leaders. We wanted to see where they worked and what their daily interactions looked like in the flesh. This enabled us to peer around the corner to see if companies really were living up to their publicly stated reputations. Regardless of where we traveled, we discovered beautiful office spaces that clearly do more than provide a roof over people's heads. Some offices were nestled inside big-city high-rises, whereas others chose character-rich suburban locations. Almost always, the location was no accident. Whether because of convenient commutes, cheap rents, or spectacular views, locations are an important part of the overall company objectives.

We asked Jules Pieri, CEO of The Grommet, about the role physical space plays in the success of the business and its meaning to the team and their customers. "When [our clients] first walked in after our move here a year and a half ago, they said, 'Oh, it's like a 3D version of the company.' You know, the brand they knew online and through the things they'd heard about us. I like that. That was the goal. I was pretty personally involved in picking this space. There are a lot of artifacts around here, a lot of salvage and vintage—things that represent manufacturing—and I picked all those out personally. So it's signaling who we are, really quickly." Pieri's story underlines how a leader can frame the culture by curating the details of the physical space. Although we discussed this in more detail in Chapter 1, it's worth making the point again. Physical space isn't just a container for your business and your team, it's a container for your brand.

"We moved into this neighborhood in an area of Portland called Central Eastside," says Marcelino Alvarez, CEO and founder of Uncorked Studios. "It's a lightweight industrial kind of neighborhood. It has a raw, warehouse-y kind of feel." The office space is on the third floor of an older building that looks like it might have been a warehouse in its previous life. On the day of our visit to Uncorked, we passed a trendy-looking restaurant setting up for the evening on the building's first floor. And across the street, a coffee-shop-meets-coworking-space was bustling with people from the neighborhood. "We moved here three years ago and had about a quarter of the space we have today. We've expanded a couple of times. For us, a few things were really amazing and unique about this building: one is the character of this neighborhood—you've got a brewery down the street, a sandwich bar across the street, a nice restaurant downstairs; we have a train, which will inevitably run through this interview—that's part of the character of Portland. It's not too polished, it's not too raw, but it's very authentic." This juxtaposition was reflected in the decor of the Uncorked office space, something Marcelino described as being a reflection of the people who work there. "If you look around the office, it's a mix of things: a nicely designed furniture piece with something that was hand-built by one of our employees. We like this mix, duality of design into something homegrown."

This aspect of the physical space Uncorked occupies is fascinating; it represents—in tangible way—the people who work there. We wondered if this influenced the culture of the company, and Marcelino described that it works on a number of levels. Not only do their people contribute to the work space in a real, useful manner (by building pieces of furniture), but the act of doing this is a manifestation of the principle of authenticity that is at the heart of the company.

"We have engineers who are also studio people. They like building things with their hands. From a visual design perspective, it means that the work that we're doing needs to present itself as an authentic thing. Don't let polish get in the way of the substance of what we're building. Culturally, it means don't lose sight of the function of what we're doing. Design for design's sake or tech for tech's sake is bad, so make sure that there's a purpose behind what we're doing."

HOW SPACE ENHANCES BRAND PERSONALITY

Probably the most important insight we came across during our leader interviews was that these physical structures are very supportive of the company's vision. Leaders felt that a thoughtfully considered physical space was an extension of their leadership style, the company culture, and the ongoing team dynamics, and thus how the office is designed and decorated should not be left to chance. Choices about decor and layout should reflect the team values. For example, at Fresh Tilled Soil, one of our values is to "Keep Things Simple." This idea has guided our choice of furniture, decor, and desk positioning. A significant portion of the office is open-plan seating, and desks are kept clutter-free to reflect the notion of simplicity. This also extends to client experiences. When a client visits the Fresh Tilled Soil offices, they are greeted by a custom-design iPad app that notifies the person they are there to meet with a simple touch of the screen. This small detail reduces the potential anxiety of a visitor when there's no receptionist to greet them at the door.

Our interviews revealed that the importance of office space cannot be underestimated for creative groups. For new companies and small groups, the need for office space might be impractical. Big-city rents make office space the second biggest expense next to salaries and wages. As companies grow, they have the means to support an office space and bring more people together under a single roof. "I think ... 10 years ago, I would have said office space was less important, and now I actually have come around to think it's quite important," says Libby Delana of Mechanica, whose team of 30 work in a beautiful building in a small coastal town in Massachusetts, "because I think there is something magical that happens, often organically, in the creative process that can't be contained to conference calls and a distinct time of day when we're all going to dial in and talk to each other about something. There is something good that happens when you're in a room together." Humans are social animals and the social interactions that happen at an office can't be ignored. It's possible to create these connections remotely, but we've seen time and time again that it's harder to do it when several of those team members are remote. "We have a big kitchen table, I call it the dining table, where there's Hershey's Kisses spilled all over, and we're all just casually talking about a client or, 'Did you all see this? Did you see the new virtual reality this and that?' There is this pollination of ideas and thinking that sometimes can't be restricted to being scheduled. So I think I've evolved. I think I used to think it was less important and I now actually personally really value the time that we're here."

It's important to point out here that physical spaces are opportunities for teams to connect socially and culturally. That doesn't mean you can't have a remote team. To the contrary, as we'll see later in this chapter, there are dozens of design groups with remote team members that are doing very well. However, even these remote teams come together from time to time to get to know each other. Whether that's done in a permanent office space or at a convenient neutral location is up to the company. Even when companies have dedicated office space, they might also choose to bring all their team members together for group meetings. Viget brings their three offices together for an annual retreat. Brian Williams, Viget's CEO, says that this is one of the most important events on the calendar from a cultural point of view. At Fresh Tilled Soil, we have a handful of remote team members. We'll often fly them in for important meetings and company get-togethers. In a recent team survey we did, these events were rated as the highest priority for cultural bonding and company morale.

THE MESSAGE OFFICE SPACE SENDS

Values, vision, and mission can also be captured in spaces. Connecting company values to the work space is an ideal hack to convey your company culture. "The physical space is our safe space for collaboration and creativity," says Nancy Lyons of FastSpot. "It's also a reflection of our brand—how we think and who we are—and it works to tell our story in a more visual, tangible way." The FastSpot office, located close to downtown Baltimore, aligns with the company's vision. As their website describes, on the average day you might find a team critiquing a design, a snoring bulldog, people discussing the potential for a zombie apocalypse, and an ample array of animated gifs flowing within HipChat. "In fact, our clients often comment on our space and the energy that is palpable within it. We really worked hard to make our spaces something our staff felt comfortable in and proud of. Spaces they wanted to inhabit and wanted to invite people into." Anyone walking through your company's doors, or looking at a photograph of your physical space, should get an immediate sense of what your business and culture is about.

As with culture (and leaders), each company has a distinct personality. Finding ways to communicate that personality to the people in that space, whether they be employees or clients, is part of a leader's job. In the same way that the clothes we wear reflect our tastes and personality, the way we design our office spaces reflects our company's taste. "Over the years, we've moved into two or three different spaces and we've outgrown them pretty quickly," says Vince LeVecchia, Partner and General Manager at Instrument in Portland. "This building was a temporary work space after we had a fire at a building in 2011, on the 4th of July. So we moved in here really quickly and it was out of hardship that this space was built. The teepee we're in right now was built to be our only conference room and has become a symbol of the company, because we just had to come together after that fire and get through it. The space has now become part of that culture."

Whether the values dictate the space or whether the space suggests which values are important, the connection is undeniable. "The new building will be interesting because it's way more polished; it's all new, it's bigger, it's multiple floors," says LeVecchia, pointing to the wide open, unstructured space they inhabit. "We've always had an open work space, so we've worked without walls. It's one of the values of the company and I think that just breeds an honesty. There's nowhere to hide, everybody can see what everyone else is doing, and everyone can hear and tell what's going on. The energy in an open work space just fuses, as opposed to walls that might separate people and keep that energy contained. Some people get annoyed by the open work space because of the noise or the lack of privacy but I think the benefits in terms of the energy and the camaraderie it breeds far outweigh the disadvantages."

FIRST WE SHAPE THE SPACE, THEN IT SHAPES US

Our interviews took us across North America and showed us a huge diversity in design tastes and work layouts. In Toronto, we visited Teehan+Lax where the layout was mostly open plan, apart from a few meeting rooms and executive offices. The main meeting room was centered in the space and surrounded by glass. This "fishbowl" design is more than just an architectural attribute of the office, it's a metaphor for their approach to design. "It's shaped a lot of who we are and how we work, in terms of the physical space," says Jon Lax, then founder and CEO of Teehan+Lax. Apart from the formal glass meeting rooms, the T+L space also had areas that could be described as casual meeting areas; soft seating and whiteboards were the key furnishings in these spaces. We saw teams sitting on couches or gathered around a whiteboard discussing projects. This type of in-person discussion is critical to the T+L creative process. "I mean no disrespect to people who evangelize remote working," says Lax. "I think that makes a lot of sense for a certain personality. For us, we enjoy coming into work and being in a group of people. We enjoy the interplay of conversation, of dialogue, of standing at a whiteboard together. For us, that works, as part of the creative process. We wanted a space that encouraged that."

Zurb founder Bryan Zmijewski describes how physical space is a daily reminder to the team of what they are doing and creating. "It is part of the celebration. You know, there's only so much you can communicate with space. Our goal was to create an environment which was open but where there are closed spaces to work in smaller teams and break off. This way, you can have an open floor plan in which serendipity can happen but which can be distracting, so when things require silence or you need to go someplace, there's places to do that. It also has an open floor plan for training, to be able to allow other people to be part of the community." Even if there is a lack of consistency in the layouts we visited, there is certainly a consistency in the desire to create spaces for collaboration and for quiet, focused time.

DESIGN LEADER AS INTERIOR DESIGNER

It was clear throughout our interviews that physical space influences the culture of the company. Although it's hard to quantify just how important physical space is to our leaders and their teams, all the design leaders we interviewed played a major role in the layout and choice of décor of their offices.

Jason VanLue, CEO of Envy Labs and previously CEO of Code School (acquired by PluralSight soon after our interview), describes the space he works in and its connection to culture. "Culture is a huge thing for us, so we purposely structured our office to support this. We have a large common area meant for anything but work—we want people to come in there and grab a beer or play Smash Bros. on the TV or just talk about things, hang out. Then, we have a dedicated work space which is still very open and very relaxed but with the intention that when you're in there, you're meant to be collaborating. It's structured in such a way that you can collaborate, but it doesn't feel quite as open as the common area. We're trying to create an environment where you don't feel like you have to be stuck in this little box cubicle all day."

In a heritage building in the Mount Pleasant neighborhood of Vancouver, we met with Sarah Tesla, founder and CEO of Make. The building that houses the studio was originally a brewery depot and the brewery still operates out of the building. Their trucks can be seen picking up and distributing beer to the community out of the back windows. "Today the building is surrounded by new condo developments but they've been able to retain the original facade and some of the original architecture, which is great. So we're in 3,000 square feet of really nice, open-concept, beautiful space." We asked Tesla how their space helps her do the job she needs to do every day. "That's such a good question, and I read recently that having high ceilings above you really does aid that sense of limitlessness and the ability to cultivate the feeling that you've got no end to your creative bounds. So I think that that helps." The Make studio certainly has high ceilings and the openness is tangible. "Being in a space where you get air and natural light, that combination just does wonders for your brain and your ability to be really focused on a task. We used to be in a very small space, about 700 square feet, shoulder to shoulder, and it was a little stifling."

At Smallbox, a branding, website design/development and marketing firm based in Indianapolis, we spoke to leader Jeb Banner about the design of their space. "We've got 20 people and we're located on the north side of town in an old library. It's a beautiful, post-Deco, early modern space with a lot of limestone and brick. It used to be a bomb shelter in the 1950s and has high ceilings and natural light. It's a nice space to work in. Physical space has become increasingly important to our firm. We used to be in a pretty small space. Our name, SmallBox, didn't actually come from where we started—but we started in a small little box, three of us with a card table for a meeting table. Then we started taking over all the offices on that floor in that building until we outgrew that and then we were able to purchase this library about a year ago."

We met with Anthony Armendariz, Partner and Experience Director at Funsize, and asked how important the physical space is to their work. "It's extremely important. I really didn't see that at first because I've always been the kind of guy that prefers to work alone at home, without people around, and the first company I ran in New York was all remote. I worked remotely for three-and-a-half years and got really used to that. When we started our first space and we had our first two team members, it kind of annoyed me that they were in my space. It took me a while to really see how physical touch points were so important to others on the team and to the business."

MOVE SPACE, MOVE CULTURE

Growing out of spaces and into new spaces has its obvious stresses. Some of these stresses will be on the culture itself. When so much attention has been given to how the space and the culture are connected, some of those considerations are about how the culture will survive after a move. Upgrading, or in some cases, downgrading, to a different space often leaves a part of the original culture behind. At Fresh Tilled Soil, we moved five times in nine years. Each time we moved, there was a shift in culture. By moving out of coworking spaces into a custom-designed office, the gritty culture of the early days was replaced by a more sophisticated culture. Attracting talent becomes easier when you have a beautifully designed office space, but you also lose some of the mission-focused dedication associated with early-stage companies.

A shift in culture prompted by a physical move was echoed by other design leaders. "I had a few concerns when we moved," says Jules Pieri at the Grommet. "Our current space is a beautiful office but when we made our first hire in this cool new space, I was worried, because the people who signed up in the old space weren't doing it for the space." Pieri reminds us that before this new space, the Grommet had been spread across three separate buildings: two Victorian houses and an office building, all within a short walking distance of each other. "There was nothing cool about it but the people were committed to the mission more than the space. I was worried that people would come in and be harder to vet for mission. Boy, when you went to that old office and you wanted to keep coming back, you meant it."

Layouts and Interior Design

The challenge of creating layouts that have multiple uses under one roof was a common theme among the top design firms we visited. "You know, we wanted open collaboration and at the same time to have fun," says Envy Labs Jason VanLue. "Fun and excellence are two of our core values, and we feel like they go hand in hand in the day-to-day operation of what we do." Dividing the space up into areas that can nurture company values is more than just an architectural choice—it's a choice that reinforces how the company behaves."

Brian Williams of Viget, who personally built furniture for his offices, describes how the architecture of the space reinforces the teams' working relationships. "The Boulder office is fairly small but it has a big open seating area and then a series of closed offices. Durham is similar. We're in the process of building our new headquarters in Virginia and we're really trying to balance the benefits of open seating, an open floor plan, but with lots of little spots for people to work. I'm very sensitive to that. We really want to make a space where you have your permanent desk, but on any given day you can find a spot—whether it's a booth, the kitchen, or a little phone closet—to sit in. It might be the big conference room with the ping-pong table or a couch in the corner—wherever you want to sit, you've got options. Flexibility is the key rather than trying to force everybody into one system, whether it's a closed office or an open seat." Flexibility is a quality we heard mentioned often in our interviews when discussing space design. Open spaces might be fashionable but they can be disruptive. Building spaces that allow for both public and private conversations are very important.

Carl White, CEO and cofounder of Think Brownstone, told us that in the early days of the business, they always imagined themselves in a brownstone. "We wanted a space that both we, as well as our clients, wanted to be at every day. A space that people didn't want to leave that was a nontraditional, beautiful space." They envisioned a space that freed them from the usual office layout that relied on cubicles, and that was, above all, comfortable. "Start with being comfortable and casually sitting around and tackling problems. I think it's very important. I think it's become who we are." Think Brownstone's current space looks like it might have once been a grand, old bank with marbled floors and pressed ceilings. The high ceilings and the large windows invite a lot of sunlight and give the office luxurious dimensions. Nothing in the decor has been left to chance. "This space is a lot grander than our first space and it had to be. As we've matured and become a bigger company, clients are expecting it from us, and it works. Clients book our conference rooms without having meetings with us, just to come hang out. That's magic, when they want to be in your space and they are drinking your beer and your coffee. We love that—that's part of our plan."

Our interviews gave us the opportunity to ask design leaders how much space affects how they work and their cultural organization. Without exception, they all affirmed the importance of office space design and culture. For those teams that meet regularly with each other and with clients, physical space communicates a lot more than culture. It reflects the brand and suggests a style of working between team members. But what about teams that are distributed or have some members that work remotely?

LEADING REMOTE TEAMS

Since physical space is such an important aspect of the work environment, what about remote workers and distributed teams? How do they make it work? We posed that question to several design leaders with remote teams, office-centered teams, or a combination of both.

On one end of the spectrum is the team at nGen Works, where the company has no centralized physical office. Although they all have their own home offices, a shared physical space has been a low priority for the team. Carl Smith, founder and President, who is based in Jacksonville, FL, has been running this distributed team for over a decade. At the time of the interview, the nGen team was in three countries and spread over five time zones. Smith feels that this approach works because nGen Works has a lot of organization autonomy. Even on a day-to-day basis, Smith is not managing his team directly; they're managing, or at least guiding, each other. Smith explains how he manages remotely without micromanaging the team. "It literally may be two hours a month. If there's a new business meeting, I'll sit in, which might be 20 minutes. They call me 'advisor' now because I know the history of the company. The team will go after a new healthcare product, and I'll be able to advise, 'We worked with this hospital, we worked with their pharmaceutical.' I can help them round out the experience in ways they may not be aware of."

Working remotely has obvious challenges for leaders. A strong working culture does wonders to keep remote people all rowing to the beat of the same drum. Several companies mentioned in this book don't have remote teams but do have multiple offices. One of these companies is Viget, which manages three locations spread across three states. The head office is just outside Washington, DC with slightly smaller offices in Durham, NC and Boulder, CO. "The HQ is about half the company and then Durham and Boulder are about evenly split with 15 or 16 [people] in each of those," explains Brian Williams, CEO of Viget. "We centralized some things like operations, but business development happens in all three offices. We have a little mix of talent in terms of project management, design, and development, which is all evenly spread across the offices. From a leadership perspective, we don't have a regional manager; rather, it's a function of the senior folks in each of those offices to help provide that local leadership."

Not requiring regional management appears to be a function of William's leadership style, which is very hands-on. In this interview and during other meetings with Williams, we were struck by the amount of time he spends with his team. In spite of the company's size, he still conducts one-on-one meetings with all his staff. "I try to travel a decent amount. I spend about a month every summer in Boulder, for example. I'll take my kids out of school and live in Boulder for a period of time and work from that office. I also try to get down to Durham as often as I can." For the companies we interviewed with more than one office, frequent travel was a part of the design leader's lives. It's not clear if this was a deliberate leadership strategy or a consequence of having distributed teams. Even when video-conferencing tools were mentioned, several leaders still chose to travel to their other offices and meet with their teams in person. "We do a weekly staff meeting where everybody's in a GoToMeeting. So we all stay connected that way. There's a lot of overlap in terms of projects, spread through the teams across all three offices, so it's not as isolated as it could be."

Another interesting side effect of having multiple offices is the opportunity for leaders to try different cultural approaches. "We do try to encourage a little bit of a unique culture in each office, so we view them as opportunities to experiment," says Williams. "That way, we can act like a 15-person company in Boulder, because it's just that little office. We're able to try some things, see if it works. If it does, we can apply it across the whole company. So in the multioffice setup, it's one of the benefits."

Greg Hoy, founder and current President of Happy Cog, focuses in on the importance of a combined team even when you have multiple offices. "Before Greg Storey and I combined our companies, he ran a very virtual company, so this is a new thing for me and I think it's more manageable to have two planets orbiting each other rather than a bunch of little asteroids all over the place." At the time of the interview, Happy Cog had two main offices: one in Philadelphia and one in Austin with a few remote team members in New York and San Francisco. "I think it's more manageable to have groups of people that you can connect with. We installed a video-conferencing system that we use to connect with each other on a daily basis. Our project teams are intermingled with people from Philly and Austin, so it is very much like one family. When we were operating separately, we'd run into turf issues but since combining we don't do that anymore. By working with combined teams, it's a one-for-all thing, which has worked out much better than I anticipated."

THE SPACE BETWEEN

Somewhere between companies that have a dedicated office space and those that are completely office-less are companies that have both physical offices and remote workers. One such company is Crowd Favorite, with US offices in New York, Denver, Los Angeles, Phoenix, Las Vegas, and international offices in Rome, Sydney, and Bucharest. Alex King, founder of Crowd Favorite and outgoing CEO at the time of our visit, believes you can have offices and remote workers but reminded us that skills development is often easier in person. "I think that physical offices can support developer growth more directly than remote environments can. Somebody can say, 'Hey, I'm having trouble with this,' and two people can turn around and hover around their desk and the solution is right there. I find that there are people that I need to coordinate with remotely, and I need to be much more intentional about reaching out to them and getting them on video and talking with them. Whereas, if I just come into the office, I feel more casually connected to all the people that I'm looking at and bumping into on the way to the kitchen."

Almost all of the companies we met with had a combination of office and remote workers, even if those remote workers were freelancers. Having flexibility with staff and skills accommodates the inevitable ups and downs of the design industry. A few design leaders are taking this idea to the extreme. One such model that allows for significant flexibility is an idea we heard referred to as the "Hollywood Model." As the name suggests, this is when a team comes together for a specific project and then go their separate ways when the project is complete. Dan Mall, CEO of SuperFriendly, has been using this Hollywood approach for several years now. He explains how the frustrations of previous projects inspired him to create a fluid design team. "I've been really fortunate to work at some great agencies and work with a lot of great people. One thing I found lacking was that sometimes I would work with people that weren't always the experts at that thing. We would work on, say, a kid's site, and I would have loved to work with an information architect that had expertise in kid's sites, but we don't always have that person on staff and I think that's one of the flaws of colocated or permanent employee models." Although this problem is not unique to Mall's firm, his approach has yet to be adopted by many design leaders.

Mall also recognized that being able to remain fluid could be a strategic differentiator for his company. "I kept thinking, how could I collect the best group of people but not have to put them on payroll? And that led me to the idea of a Hollywood model. It works in the same way that a director staffs a film. They don't always use the same actors; they get the actors that are right for the roles. The teams scale up and down depending on the project. There might be projects where the team is as small as one or two people, and others where the team might be as large as 16 people, although we found the sweet spot is usually around four to six. Generally, these mid-size projects are web redesigns and the makeup is pretty similar. I'd heard of a couple of people running companies that way and I figured it would be a good thing to try out. So far, so good."

Clearly, Mall is pushing the boundaries of team organization and the need for space. Like Mall's Hollywood model, the description of his work space feels a lot like a movie studio. "When I moved back to Philly from Brooklyn, I moved to an old church that we renovated. So my wife, my kids, and I live upstairs, and underneath my house I have a 30,000 square foot studio that I work out of. Right now, I have three apprentices and we all work out of the studio." Combining work and family under one roof seems unusual in today's society, but it hasn't always been that way. In previous generations, most of the city and town shop owners would live above their stores or workspaces. Times might have changed but many of our leaders still like the idea of a walkable commute, which suggests Mall might be on to something with his converted church space.

This Hollywood model popped up in various forms during our research. Bringing together the best qualified people for the project makes sense for a lot of design firms and groups. "We can't afford to keep dozens of people on the bench waiting for the right project to come along that needs all of them," says Christine "Chris" Quinn of eHouse Studios in the charming city of Charleston, SC. "Our clients don't expect it either. They want us to be the GCs [general contractors] for the project and provide the strategic direction for the creative work, but they don't expect us to have photographers, videographers, content editors, or writers on staff all the time." Apart from getting the best people for the job, this model works also because most small- to medium-sized agencies don't have the financial muscle to keep a large staff of secondary creative people on the payroll. It's nothing new, though. For years, larger agencies have been bringing in outside talent for projects that require specialist skills. As digital products integrate more with rich media, we can expect to see content and data specialists being brought into the mix more frequently.

"Essentially, the idea at its core was that we would have very little, if any at all, creative talent under our roof," says Libby Delana, cofounder of Mechanica, located in the picturesque seaside town of Newburyport, MA. "Meaning, we don't have our directors. We don't have directors of photography, or photographers, or sound people under our roof at Mechanica. Honestly, to build a brand, you potentially might need all those people. What we began to feel was there was no way to have an entire suite or portfolio of the right creative people on hand at any given moment, to really put together a compelling plan for any client. For some clients, it might be interior design. They may be moving to a new space and we have a new positioning and a new way of talking about the brand." To solve this problem, Delana and her team deconstructed the traditional agency model so they have no creative talent in-house other than creative directors. Although the leadership and strategic directors remain consistent, each client has a unique team built around their proposed solution. "So Client A may need a big TV and radio and podcasts, and a lot of photography, while Client B may need mostly web talent," explains Delana. "We call it the *endless creative hallway*, meaning that I, as a creative director, instead of walking down the hall and looking left and right, and poking my head into somebody's door and saying, 'Hey, are you available to work on this account today? or 'What's your timeline like?', I go out into the world and bring together on that client's piece of business the best people in the world."

FINAL WORDS

If one thing's clear, it's that there's no single answer to how an office should be set up. The design leaders have their personal preferences, but they all agree that having a physical space to collaborate in can be a huge benefit. Even permanently remote teams meet a few times a year to discuss strategies and process. These annual or semiannual gatherings are a reminder that design teams need social interaction. In spite of the new telecommuting economy, humans still value each other. Whether the team is all in a single office or spread across the world, the key element is having the team connected in a way that improves collaboration. Even companies with proven models have to consider other organizational models.

"We are distributed in a way that we are across three offices, but all three offices are on-location offices. Meaning, we don't have employees that work from home or remotely," says Aurimas Adomavicius of Devbridge, which has about 150 employees in three locations. "For us, that's very important. I've even written about this. It's very important for us that employees are centralized in these locations and they have educational tracks filled out. They have on-location managers that they can talk to. So from an operation standpoint—onboarding new people, hiring new people, and so on and so forth—we believe that being on location is very important. Now having said all of that, still, when we work, we use teams that are blended teams of individuals across all offices."

KEY TAKEAWAYS

- There are no black-and-white solutions to physical space—they are more like shades of gray.
- Successful office layouts tend to have healthy combinations of both open and closed, as well as casual and formal spaces.
- The company's personality and brand should be allowed to shine through in the choice of location, space layout, and decor.
- When moving to a new location, consider how that will affect culture, and try to preserve the elements that work.

- Something as simple as providing extra seats for staff to engage in informal conversation around desks can increase communication between team members.

- Don't be afraid to move people around the office from time to time. This allows new connections between team members to be created.

- Remote teams need frequent and routine communication to stay bonded and aligned.

- Hiring people that are already good self-managers makes remote working easier.

Personal Growth and Finding Balance

Introduction

No successful project gets done without meeting deadlines, staying on budget, and managing lots of different people. There's a lot on the line. For the leaders of high-performing design groups and million-dollar design firms, these pressures are felt daily. Seemingly never-ending deadlines, constant people management, and strategic thinking in an ambiguous tech landscape are part of the territory. Seeking insights into how design leaders deliver on these demands while remaining balanced and focused was one of the motivations for writing this book. As it is with other CEOs and founders, the strategies and tactics of how to find balance and personal growth is always on our mind.

The theme of this chapter might seem more appropriate to being included in a self-help book. The reality is that the personal growth and mental health of the leader is inexplicably linked to the success of any business. Without exception, all of the design leaders we met with felt that ongoing personal growth and leading a balanced life were critical to their success as company or team leaders. Exploring the habits, routines, and rituals of these leaders gave us insight into the inner workings of their paths to success. Their perspectives, hard-earned lessons, and strategies will give you a renewed appreciation for the attention required to lead a balanced lifestyle and the connection to a successful design business.

Finding the Right Focus

"I'm CEO, so my customer really is my team. I'm making sure that everybody who works here can achieve and become the best that they are." This comment from Dominic Bortolussi, cofounder of The Working Group, is incredibly insightful. The simplicity of this statement belies the importance of the impact it can have on a design leader's actions. "Through that exploration, I discovered that my real customer is not my clients; my customer is my team. That was an interesting shift because I'd always assumed that my customer was my clients—the people that I was building software for." Bortolussi reflects on the insight and how it led him to change the way he leads his organization. "That was a not-so-subtle shift. My recognition of my type of leadership has evolved over the past few years. I discovered that I'm a leader of meritocracy, a democratic type of leader, a leader who asks opinions of other people and then expects them to step up; not an autocratic leader. Not a 'me first' leader. Not a top-down leader."

Understanding where their strengths lie is a breakthrough moment for design leaders. Knowing how to put those strengths to work for the benefit of the team is another breakthrough step. "I do everything else that needs to be done, all the business things. All the hats that need to be worn, I wear those," says Marty Haught, founder of Haught Works, a small development team based in Boulder, CO. "I recognized at one point when we were at nine people that I was doing a lot less coding and a lot more management. I recognized that to continue on that path or get larger would mean to hire people that would do these other things. I really didn't want to do that. I wanted to have smaller teams that didn't require me to be 100% management." Haught is talking about that moment when leaders realize they need to be true to their limits. Growing your company, and thus growing into a different leadership role, is a requirement of success. Whether the company is big or small matters less than whether the leader is clear about their own path and the path of the company. Personal growth doesn't depend on the size of the company or team, but there does seem to be a correlation with maturity.

Finding your place in the team can only happen when the team has found a focus for its collective efforts. Being able to put guidelines around who you are as a design group helps the team members define their ideal contributions. When clearly described, this focus trickles through the organization and allows the design team to know how they should behave when new projects come their way. "The one thing about us is we say 'no' first," says Instrument's COO, Vince LeVecchia. "The trap is to say yes to everything in a creative agency, get the work in, figure it out later. With us, if you start out by saying no to the mediocrity or the thing that just looks good, you really then curate all the work you do." This hyper-focused thinking was common among mature leaders and their organizations.

Not just focus, but focus with a purpose. It can be tempting to say yes to everything that comes your way. Certainly, when you're starting out, you might have to do just that.

"We took the easy road that was in front of us," reflects Steven Fitzgerald of Habanero Consulting. "We got caught up in thinking that it was about doing something for a client that would help them out of a problem, rather than focusing on stuff we would be awesome at. That's the cycle we go through and that's the lesson." Losing focus or allowing distractions to determine the path was a lesson often learned the hard way but often the most valuable lesson leaders reported on. "When we live outside our purpose, nothing works well. I'm not saying it's easy to understand and just stick there. It's very hard. That's the whole challenge."

These hard lessons in finding focus appear to be consistent with the changing demands of a growing business. The longer your business has been around, the more distractions there will be. Successful leaders recognize this escalation and counter with increased focus. That often means ignoring opportunities or turning away certain projects. From personal experience, I can attest to how difficult this is. I've made numerous investments in side projects and new service offerings that have not borne any fruit. The key is to surround yourself with smart advisors and partners that can help you stay the course. Recently I've invested in operations people that act as gatekeepers and protect me from distractions so I remain focused. The rewards have been significant. This book, and the one before it, would not have been possible without those people playing interference to my distractions.

Partners and Support

Entrepreneur and author Jim Rohn once said that you are the average of the five people you spend the most time with. This appears to hold a lot of truth for our design leaders, too. Surrounding yourself with a great team makes dealing with the stresses of running a high-functioning design team so much easier. Another point worth making here is that a supporting team isn't restricted to the group of people you work with directly. Our design leaders almost always referenced their families, clients, and mentors in our conversations.

"First of all, I prioritize the things at work that make it not just tolerable but enjoyable," says Brian Williams, of Viget. "Hiring people that I love to work with is one of the things. We also try to be as selective as we can with clients so we can be working on things that we're passionate about." For Viget and many of the other companies we visited, taking the time to select the best team members and filtering for the ideal clients made the work tasks easier. Although this overlaps with our chapter on talent, it's worthwhile reaffirming the importance of having the right people in your organization. Almost everything design leaders talk about in their work and home lives comes back to people. Support, culture, inspiration, and excellence all relate to the people that design leaders have in their orbits.

For any leadership position to be successful, there has to be a significant amount of support. Not just the support of the organization but the support of family and friends. Surrounding yourself with people who really know you and can help you find that balance even when you think you're lost. "Work-life balance is hard," adds Uncorked's Marcelino Alvarez. "I think my wife's been a great supporter of what we've been doing. She ... is in advertising, so understanding the industry that we're in certainly helps." Gesturing to his phone, "There are times when I get the nudge of 'turn it off' and I think it's a good nudge to have. I think that the balance is more of an internal one where I'll start thinking about something. It'll be in the back of my mind. I'm thinking of something else. I'm not here and present. I'm nodding my head but really I'm just trying to crack this thing. And that's hard because people who don't know you might think, 'Wow, he's really nodding his head a lot.' But I think people who do know you are like, 'Stop. Stop thinking about the thing. I know that you're thinking about that meeting or that conversation or something at work.' Be honest with yourself. Taking a day to work from home or turning it off on the weekend and just hitting a reset point I think is really important."

WHERE THE INSPIRATION AND SUPPORT COMES FROM

"A lot of experimentation, trial and error," says Sarah Tesla about finding the right place to get support and inspiration. "I am fortunate. My husband is a founder of a digital creative agency in Vancouver and has been doing it for a decade, and he's got two partners. So he's been a limitless resource for me, which has been great." Family and friends are undoubtedly where design leaders turn but not everyone is married to a seasoned pro. What Tesla says next is the clue to the mindset that seems to set successful leaders apart. "In honesty, I really am pretty humble about what I know and what I don't know." This humility and willingness to learn is the key. Being in a constant state of learning prevents the top design leaders from getting stuck. Whether they are leaning on a partner, spouse, or a team member, they are universally coachable. "I rely a lot on my team in that sense, to be experts in what they do and allow me to try and figure out what I have to do," concludes Tesla.

For most of the leaders we spoke to, support is at their office every day. In spite of the importance of family, friends, and external advisors, their closest support comes in the form of their partners. "There are a lot of leaders here," says Dominic Bortolussi of The Working Group. "I also have three other partners. There are four partners in the business and they are each a phenomenal leader in their own area." It's worth hearing from Bortolussi what each partner does to understand how they compliment each other. "We have Chris Eben here. [He] is very visible in the community, does a lot of speaking engagements, is very active in our business development. So his leadership is very visible and [he] is sort of the traditional corporate leader who is out there speaking and pointing the direction. Andres is also a phenomenal leader. He leads all of our project operations and has amazing empathy and ability to connect with people. His leadership is really through example, through his amazing communication abilities. Jack is our technical director and his technical leadership is through example, by doing. He's perhaps the most dedicated worker I know. He puts his head down and solves problems with people, and he's getting really good at incorporating other people into a problem-solving system."

As illustrated by Bortolussi's description of his partners, there's a lot of specialization for each area of leadership. The partners use their respective strengths to support each other and the business as a whole. Unlike the popular media's love affair with the lone leader, the reality is that most businesses need some kind of partnership to be successful. "Fortunately, we have complementary strengths and mine tend to be operational," says Tiffany Farriss, one of the two CEOs at Palantir. "I'm very good on the finance side. I manage the books and I'm also the more technically minded of the two of us. So for the more technical engagements, I'll go in and pitch those. George is excellent at vision and strategy for the company as well as communication, getting our brand and communicating those things. So there's been kind of a clear division. He tends to work on the company with the exception of finance, and then I tend to work on our clients and then the finance piece."

Another leading design firm, CloudFour in Portland, OR, has a similar partnership, which started out with four partners but now is down to three. "We've worked with each other for seven years. And Lyza and John have worked together longer," tells Jason Grigsby, CEO and cofounder. "John has since left and started another startup. Now Lyza, Aileen, and I run the business on a day-to-day basis."

Grigsby points out how the lives of the partners are not limited to what's going on at work. "The things that are going on in our personal lives impact what's going on in the business, whether we like it or not. Being able to figure out how to find alignment ends up being a big thing. And we've had periods of the company's history where we weren't aligned, and things were really rough. But in times when we're aligned at a high level, all of the small stuff on a day-to-day basis usually works itself out."

Grigsby cautions with a wry grin, "I think if you've got people that you've worked with for quite some time, you could still screw it up." In business, nothing is guaranteed, even with great partners to support you. Markets change, trends pass, and new technology shows up at every turn. So how else do design leaders reduce the risk of making mistakes and creating positive outcomes?

Designing Balance

Creating the outcomes you want is not something you leave to chance. Successful design leaders are used to crafting solutions for their clients and they seem to use these techniques in their own lives as well. In their daily lives, many of them take a design-thinking approach to how work and home life fits together. Deliberately designing your daily routine instead of being reactive was a common approach. For some, this can be as simple as choosing to live close to the office to avoid a stressful commute, but mostly it's about developing a routine that allows for personal enrichment while also dealing with the demands of company leadership.

Successful leaders acknowledge that growth and harmony are also a product of timing. The needs of the business change over time, and so do the opportunities to learn new skills. Unlike riding a bike, finding the right balance is a lesson our leaders have to keep learning, because the context is always changing. What works when they're running a company of five people is very different from the things that are needed when there are 50 people to lead.

"I think it's a yin-yang type of thing," says Bryan Zmijewski, of finding balance in personal and professional endeavors. "You're going to go through periods where you're going to get lots of inputs that you weren't expecting and you have to deal with them." Zmijewski has lead his company, Zurb, through Silicon Valley's most challenging decade. He likens finding harmony in his life to ocean fishing. "There are times where you want to set course but you're just holding on because the waters are turbulent. In these moments, you don't try fishing. When the waters are calm, you go fishing. That's hard to learn because oftentimes we become impatient in wanting to create things when there's really not circumstances or an environment for them to be successful. So I think the lesson I learned in probably the last few years is that you have to be patient."

"I've always loved being an employee and I was really fortunate to have great bosses. So I never felt that I was lacking in that." SuperFriendly's Dan Mall describes how his past experiences helped him deliberately craft a design firm around his lifestyle needs. "Really, the motivation to find balance came when I had kids. I just wanted to stay home with my wife and kids a lot. I thought it would be selfish to ask any company I worked for to let me do that. The places that I worked, the cultures just weren't really good for that; it would have been really selfish of me to do that. So for me it was a good time to see if I could just at least work from home and spend more time with my family and then figure out how to sustain myself and my family through that." In most modern economies, the idea of freelancing or working from home is nothing new. Mall has taken this concept to the next step by starting with family priorities and designing a business around that. The irony is that even designers don't use their design skills to craft their careers. Successful design leaders show us that it's necessary to approach lifestyle and careers as a design problem to be solved with many of the same tools and exercises used in their everyday work.

Viget's Brian Williams describes how his decision to craft some of the aspects of his business routines around his family priorities has had a positive impact on his overall life balance. "In terms of making sure the work part is enjoyable, it's a typical time-management discipline-type stuff. I'm fortunate that I can walk to the office so I don't have a big long commute. I can be around in the morning, get the kids on the bus, be home in time for dinner every night, that kind of thing."

Williams adds additional perspective: "The business is successful enough and we have enough of a team where we've delegated stuff and spread the workload. In most cases, I don't have to work weekends like I did for the first five years." It might not be realistic for many to start out with a company that can provide the support for all the leader's career criteria. Design businesses can take time to grow to the point where the team is large enough to do what Williams describes. He cautions that it required effort and a long-term vision to get where he is today. "Getting the thing off the ground seemed endless. I'm not driven by financial success. I mean the company is financially successful in every measure but I'm not targeting some huge exit or something along those lines. My goal is to create a business that is sustainable and enjoyable for me and for the staff and for everybody that's involved. We've decided we can do something we want to do for the next 20 years while we raise the kids, remain a part of the community, and stay connected to all these things that I love to do." Williams summarizes his approach and suggests a strategy that puts long-term outcomes before pure business goals, "If you change the dynamic and say, 'I want to create this sustainable work environment,' I think that can change the way you balance your time and your life."

Designing a balanced life isn't something that has to wait for the company or team to grow large. Instilling values that promote balance can happen at any point. The key here is that there's a deliberate approach to finding a way to get the work done and not burn out. The design leaders we met with have learned that by designing their lives for a positive outcome, they flatten out the inevitable bumps in the road. They actively seek out time to spend with family and friends. In fact, 45% of design leaders consider time with family the best stress relief.

"We used to think about the concept of work-life balance but I hate that term. It feels like a zero sum game," remarks Steven Fitzgerald, CEO of Habanero Consulting Group in Vancouver. "We've evolved our thinking about the term. Now we have a value based on harmony. You should create an environment where you can experience passion in the different parts of your life that really matter. It's very temporal and it's very specific. For me, it's things like riding my bike, it's Habanero, it's my kids and my family and my community. If I can deeply engage in those things and experience passion in them, I take energy from that and I put it into the other ones."

Fitzgerald makes the distinction between harmony and work-life-balance. "The concept of work-life-balance conveys the feeling that you're going to be a deadbeat dad and work hard at work, being a successful businessman this month. That's not the way I see it. When I had a great night with the kids, I show up at work better the next day. When I have a good ride into work or a good ride on the weekend, it helps me be a better dad. It helps me be a better partner to my wife. It helps me be better at Habanero. That passion fuels the other things. I think it's the opposite of a zero sum game." This insight is of paramount importance. You can't sustain good design leadership if you're not taking care of your mental, emotional, and physical health. Making these things a priority and carving out the time to achieve harmony isn't just a nice-to-have, it's a requirement of successful leadership. Put family and exercise into your schedules before they fill up with meetings and other distractions.

Designing a harmonious career starts with the smallest elements. Organizing each day and week adds together to create more manageable months and years. "I think the other piece for me, really, comes down to just sort of how I've kind of organized myself and my days," says Scott Baldwin of Yellow Pencil. "I tend to use a good system to plan around my tasks. Knowing what I need to do and what I need to achieve for that week gives me a head start. I think it's kind of a bit of a bastardization between a 'get things done' and kind of a Stephen Covey approach. It follows the idea or concept that we need to make space for these bigger things and objectives in our lives, which are our priorities. Rocks, in the Covey[1] language."

"I see it as flow, not balance," says Jeb Banner of SmallBox. "There's balance on a moment-to-moment level, where you need to make sure you're managing stress and activity and all that, but to me, life is about flow. It's about things feeding each other and creating positive energy in both directions, work to life. I don't think those are going to become any more separated going forward." This last point is extremely important. Modern design leaders, or any contemporary leadership role, isn't going to look like the leadership roles of the past. Your dad's-era CEO who clocked out at 5 p.m. and never got an email at noon on a Saturday is now a quirky history lesson. Today's leaders are inextricably connected to their work, wherever they are. Smartphones and mobile devices blur the lines between work and play. Banner's point about the lack of separation is something all our design leaders deal with every day. Instead of pretending there is a clear line between work and everything else, the most successful leaders acknowledge the vagueness and embrace the integration.

---

1 Dr. Stephen R. Covey, *First Things First*. For those not familiar with the metaphor repeated by Covey, it goes something like this: a man stood in front of a group of high-powered overachievers and said, "Okay, time for a quiz." Then he pulled out a large wide-mouthed mason jar and set it on a table in front of him. He produced about a dozen fist-sized rocks and carefully placed them, one at a time, into the jar. When the jar was filled to the top and no more rocks would fit inside, he asked, "Is this jar full?" Everyone in the class said, "Yes." Then he said, "Really?" He reached under the table and pulled out a bucket of gravel. Then he dumped some gravel in and shook the jar causing pieces of gravel to work themselves down into the spaces between the big rocks. Then he smiled and asked the group once more, "Is the jar full?" By this time the class was onto him. "Probably not," one of them answered. "Good!" he replied. And he reached under the table and brought out a bucket of sand. He started dumping the sand in and it went into all the spaces left between the rocks and the gravel. Once more he asked the question, "Is this jar full?" "No!" the class shouted. Once again he said, "Good!" Then he grabbed a pitcher of water and began to pour it in until the jar was filled to the brim. Then he looked up at the class and asked, "What is the point of this illustration?"

THE IMPORTANCE OF EXERCISE

Exercise came up in our conversations almost every time—either the importance of it or the frustration of not getting enough. This book probably doesn't need to describe the importance of exercise in our lives, but what is relevant to this book is the large percentage of design leaders that credit exercise with stress relief. Whether their preference was golf, running, cycling, yoga, or simply walking while on their frequent phones calls, they are inserting exercise into their days. For some it was a deliberate habit, for others an opportunity to socialize while burning calories, and for still others it was a way to escape the constant buzz of their devices. Sustaining a busy schedule starts with having the energy to do everything that's planned for, and more. Leaving physical health to chance is a sure-fire way for leaders to run out of energy and focus when they need it most.

"I like running," says Marcelino Alvarez when we asked him how he gets disconnected from the constant lure of the smartphone and into the detox zone. "For me, running two, three times a week really helps. You don't have to carry a piece of technology with you. You can't read an email while you're running. Aerobic exercise helps you to free up brain cells to think about problems. It's nice to digest ideas while you run." Running was a favorite among several of the design leaders for the reasons given by Alvarez. The upside to running, hiking, or cycling is that it allows these design leaders to either check out completely or ruminate on their challenges without the constant interruption of device notifications. By choosing activities that gave them a chance to check out a little, they were often, sometimes subconsciously, finding ways to rise above the day-to-day fray and slip into a meditative state. Alvarez continues to make the point about creating time for activities that get you out of the daily effort, "I like photography and I like fishing, too. Basically anything that forces me to get out and enjoy the water, the sun, especially in the summers here, is a good escape."

"I exercise a lot. That's become very critical in my years," says Scott Baldwin, Head of UX at Yellow Pencil. "I tend to run about at least three or four days a week. So that physical aspect of things, getting out and clearing my head, is a really important part of doing good work here." Baldwin, who is based in Vancouver, explains how important routine is in keeping stress at bay. "It's become part of the ritual. It has its ebbs and flows, like when my wife travels and I have to travel, or something like that." Having a way to frequently blow off some steam or just get the blood flowing was a common thread in the interviews. Leaders can't be expected to stay focused without some way to recharge the batteries.

"I do some yoga and some meditation," says Jeb Banner of SmallBox. "I need to do more of that. I generally do that two or three times a week, along with some exercise. I take a lot of walks when the weather permits. [I have an] elliptical at home that I use." If yard sales are anything to go by, Banner might be the only person that actually uses their elliptical at home. When we asked Aurimas Adomavicius of Devbridge how he finds harmony and balance in his life, he didn't hesitate for a second. "Just a lot of drugs." Then he chuckles and dismisses his comment. "I've found that exercise is incredibly important. Specifically, running is very, very important for managing my stress level." After hearing so many of these anecdotes, it was no surprise that 62% of design leaders reported using exercise as their primary way to relieve stress.

The physiological rewards of exercise are well understood. We all know the benefits but often struggle to develop these good habits. Making sure that physical exercise finds it's way into their busy schedules, design leaders often rely on a combination of internal and external motivators. "My wife is a personal trainer, so she forces me to exercise," laughs Dan Mall. "And so as often as we can, she tries to get me to play racquetball with her because she really loves playing racquetball, so we've been really getting into that lately." Having a partner, spouse, or friend to nudge you in the right direction is often all our design leaders need. Another way to make exercise part of your day is to connect it to the things you're already committed to. "I am a walker or a pacer. I can walk for miles and miles," says Nancy Lyons of FastSpot. "I'm not a runner or a biker, but I walk. I have walking meetings. I'll walk around blocks on calls. I'll walk on the walking work station. I'll walk after work. Or late at night when all the houses are sleepy."

Walking meetings and standing desks were very common tactics used by the design leaders. Making walking or other forms of exercise part of the company culture is a way to integrate it into everyday activities. "I like playing basketball so every once in a while, I have friends that will organize a three-on-three basketball tournament, so as much as I can, I try to do that," says Mall. "Releasing those endorphins in that way is just really, really great." It's probably not too presumptuous to suggest that if you're not making exercise and healthy living a priority then it'll be harder to achieve success in leadership. Scheduling time for healthy activity almost has to come first. If leaders don't carve out time ahead of their weeks, then without fail that time will fill up with something else. The foundation has to be set.

ALL WORK AND NO PLAY

Not all design leaders choose to sweat their stress away. At least a quarter of those interviewed preferred frequent vacations as their ideal stress reliever, while another quarter said that they would hit the bar after a tough day. This time at the bar is mostly about making time for friends. After exercise, time with friends and vacations were the most mentioned outlets for stress. This balance between work and play doesn't look the same for each leader. Some choose to blow off steam daily or weekly, while others wait until they are completely burned out. "I believe that to be successful, you have to work a lot," says Devbridge's Adomavicius. "I don't have the mentality that you just work eight hours a day and that's enough." Adomavicius describes an almost as extreme but personally effective strategy to finding balance: "What I've found is I become busy and allow for some burn out. Then I take a big break. I believe that there's an engagement curve that looks like a sine amplitude, where essentially, you as an individual, you gain focus in these intense sprints and you're very effective when you gain that focus. But you can only be super effective and work 12 hours, 14 hours a day for a limited sprint, then you have to wind down and you have to decompress." This approach is extreme but not as uncommon as we first expected. Working intense hours for months at a time and then disengaging completely to recharge was mentioned several times. The Working Group's Dominic Bortolussi took an extended sabbatical after several years of intense work. "It was fantastic. I would recommend at least four months. I began with three months and it was clear that I needed more time, so I extended to four months." Bortolussi spent much of his time completely disconnected from the office. Apart from a handful of check-in calls, he was "off the grid." His sabbatical included riding his motorcycle to L.A. from Toronto, surfing and playing music in Bali, studying meditation in Thailand, and studying yoga in India.

"I prefer having these really aggressive sprints and then good decompression moments after them. I have time off where I travel, or I do something where I'm decompressing and not as engaged with work," explains Adomavicius. "I found that if I can do that, I'm much more creative and productive in those work sprints versus having a normalized engagement level of, 'Oh, I worked the regular number of hours a day for four, six months,' and then take a vacation or something." Finding a rhythm that works for your particular style is ideal. As we've said before, no leader is the same. Each design leader needs to find a pattern that keeps him engaged and let's him recharge when necessary. "I think there's some type of rhythm in nature that I just synchronize to, and I just need to be able to detect the phase I'm in," says Marcelino Alvarez. "If I'm finding that I'm burned out and not as engaged and not as creative, I just need to step back a little bit and give myself time. When I see that interest peaking again, then I need to really hit it and work a lot of hours and work weekends. Because I know that in that period when I'm most engaged and most excited, I will produce the best results. That's my mentality."

If reducing stress is the goal, then Adomavicius and others feel they are going to achieve this when they deal with the issues head on and work even harder. "I really enjoy the company and the growth," says Velir CEO Dave Valliere. "There's definitely times that are extremely stressful, whether we're dealing with onboarding a new client, kicking off a new project, or maybe there are some issues that we're working through with a client, or working through with internal staff, or those growth pains that I was talking about before. What I find is during these stressful times, I work even more. It seems crazy, but I think that the more time that I'm spending focusing on these areas and the more attention that I'm paying to the issues, the more I am reducing my stress. I would imagine that there's a lot of folks that are in these positions that feel more anxious when they're away from work than when they're in it, regardless of what's going on at the time in the organization. That's definitely something that I've felt over the years is that my anxiety levels go down when I'm more actively engaged in what's happening. For sure, my wife hates that aspect. Even when we're on vacation, I'm still going to be sending email, still responding to things. But I think that if I didn't, I would feel more anxious."

Design leaders often attribute their desire to stay connected to the business as a responsibility to their team. "I think that it's the responsibility that I feel to the rest of staff that's driving me to want to spend more time on a problem," says Valliere. "I need to be able to think about the different angles to this particular situation that we're dealing with. I think if I was more disconnected from them, I would feel more anxious. So it's actually just being more involved with work that is actually what's making me relaxed." Whether your style is to pull back or dive deeper, the insight is that each leader needs to find their own rhythm. Learning to read their patterns gives these design leaders some power over their stress. By combining that insight with their individual remedies, the design leaders are able to stay creative and energized.

Planning for a Harmonious Future

Design isn't just a solution for their daily work. Design is also a solution for how design leaders craft their lives. An unavoidable part of designing any solution is the testing phase. Having a solution in your head is one thing, but getting that solution out into the real world and tested against harsh realities is quite another thing. "When I first started SuperFriendly while working from home, I thought, I'm going to have a very strict schedule," says Dan Mall. "I'm going to work 9:00 to 5:00. Nine o'clock, I'm going to clock in—no earlier. Five o'clock, I'm going to clock out—no later. That just didn't work for me. Work just bleeds in and out of that. My kids would come downstairs and want to play, and I would just be angry at them because this was work time and I had to get work done."

"So what I do now is the opposite, where I work a really long day with really long breaks in between. So I get up at 5 a.m., and every morning I work from 5:00 to 7:00 because it's quiet and that's my most productive time, when I'm waking up and sort of becoming more alert for the day and starting to think about the day. And then, from about 7:00 to 10:00, I go have breakfast with my kids, drop them off at school, hang out with my wife. Start work around 10:00, 10:30 and then I work until about 3:00 or 4:00 when my kids come home. Come downstairs, we play for an hour, half an hour, something like that and then I work until 7:00 or 8:00. So I'm technically, like, at my desk from 5 a.m. until 8 p.m., which is a really long day but I take a lot of long breaks in between. That has actually helped me to have more balance than if I've been having a strict schedule. So I find that's working for me lately."

Not all planned solutions need to be complicated lifestyle experiments. Sometimes all you need is a way to get through your to-do list with a little more momentum. "Think of it as of marginal gains, or small-serve, incremental pieces," suggests Scott Baldwin at Yellow Pencil. "I tend to focus on the three to five things I need to do this week. I think about how to involve other people in the tasks. I do a lot of planning ahead of time, to make sure I'm already thinking about next week's calendar and next week's meeting today, not next week." Baldwin's approach is to narrow down the focus of his effort to the most important items on the list. He backs this up with finding ways to get help and possibly even delegate if necessary. "I ask myself, 'what are the things that we're doing this week to move those forward?' This sense of incremental gain over time is empowering. People with a big goal, or a big objective, start to freak out and wonder how the hell are they going to do that. If you break it down into small pieces, it's not so scary. You ask, how about this week we work on this proposal? And next week, we maybe go talk to this client. And two weeks from now, we maybe do this. Over time, and incrementally, we might get to that big goal." This strategy isn't unique but its simplicity belies its effectiveness. Breaking goals down makes them accessible and manageable without diluting the motivation of having an exciting challenge ahead. Having a strategy, any strategy, provides peace of mind. Baldwin adds with a smile, "I've always been a zero inbox kind of guy, or just about, but I think a lot of it is just coming down to having a clear head and taking clear actions at the right times."

RULES AND ROUTINE

"I've been very, very strict in how I manage when I'm working and when I'm not," says Ross Beyeler, CEO of Growth Spark. "There are always exceptions. Every rule has an exception, but most of time, I will not start work before 10 a.m. and once I leave the office, my email is off. I will not check email when I'm outside of the office and I won't start checking again until 10 a.m. the next day. As soon as I'm done on Friday, around 5 p.m., I'm totally inaccessible over the weekend." In our observations, this discipline is not rare but tends to be associated with more mature leaders. Not everyone we spoke to drew hard lines between work and the rest of their lives. For some design leaders who prefer staying somewhat connected, it might not be as simple as turning off your phone or ignoring email for days at a time. For many design leaders, there is a middle ground, where weaving all aspects of work and life into each other is better than completely separating church and state.

Defining the times and spaces for work and then communicating that clearly to the people around you is necessary if you want boundaries. In the absence of boundaries, clients or staff will simply assume you're available. This goes for significant others and family, too. "We've been doing it so long at this point, it's almost routine," says Tiffany Farriss, co-CEO of Chicago-based Palantir, "and what I realized is that balance isn't about carving separate time for different things." Farriss, who runs the 35-person firm alongside her husband, George DeMet, feels that it's about integrating things in a way that doesn't compromise their children or their personal relationship. "So we have these times that are off bounds to talk about work stuff, unless it's an urgent matter. The dinner table, for example. No phones at the dinner table, and after 9 o'clock at night, you just don't talk about work. We try to keep our weekend contained, but if we need to, we respect that the other person might not be in that same place. So if there's something I'm working on or if there's something that is really bothering me that I'm trying to solve ... and I need his help, if it's outside of normal work hours, I ask him if he can help me with it and when might be a good time for him. I have to be respectful of his personal time the same way I would be of any of my other colleagues."

Farriss's insight is great guidance for leaders whose partnerships go beyond the office. In partnerships between spouses, you have to treat your partner as you would anybody else. Assuming they want to talk about work after hours is disrespectful to the other person's time. Discussing when and where it's okay to discuss work helps set the boundaries in a healthy way for everyone. This might also extend to comanagers and staff. Letting them know when you are available after hours or on weekends helps them understand when they can bug you with questions or updates. Using the tech available helps, too. Calendars and out-of-office responses tell people when you're not around. I book time for exercise and family time into my calendar so my team doesn't accidentally book me for a meeting during those times. Being explicit about where your boundaries are is helpful to the people around you and gives them clear guidance about when you're available and when you're not.

ACQUIRING NEW SKILLS

Finding harmony often means growing skills. Our conversations with design leaders almost always included questions about their personal approach to growing as leaders. We already knew from our own experience that growth as a leader is often a consequence of the challenges we face. These external influences are certainly not consistent. They come in waves.

This seems obvious, but we wanted to know what they are thinking about or doing during these ups and downs that helped them improve as leaders. Dan Mall of SuperFriendly says, "I take very calculated risks. I think the skill that I lack most is bravery. That's been really hard to work on for me because I've always taken risks that I know have no consequence. I've never really taken a risk that I didn't know had no consequences. I've never really risked if it weren't going to pan out. So I think that's a thing that I could work on and definitely learn more about. I think I like to work with people that want to learn stuff. I find that even though I hire people that are really good at what they do, if they don't come into the project thinking that they're going to learn something, or not expecting to learn something, and just expecting like, 'I'm going to execute and get out,' I find that it's not interesting. We do good work, I think, and those projects end up good, but it's not interesting if we're not learning something together. The people that I really love working with most are the people that have no idea how to do the thing that we're going to do, and then figure it out along the way. I'm very attracted to those people. People that come in and are just like, 'I've no idea on how to go about this, but I'm very confident in my own learning abilities that by the end of it I will be an expert.' I'm very drawn to those kinds of people."

Some leaders learn through trial and error, while others learn by watching or listening to others. The best leaders balance these two approaches. Going to the source of the knowledge is something we tried to do with this book. Either approach brings results, but the latter brings results faster. The caveat is that the leader needs to know where their strengths and weakness lie so they know what gaps to fill. Listening to advice from a mentor on a skillset that you have no strength for might be a waste of time. Knowing which skills need your attention focuses your search for solutions and insights. "Part of it was delegation," says Dominic Bortolussi of The Working Group, "by leaning on my partners to be the full leaders in areas that I wasn't as good at. The other part of it was discovering what I am good at. Knowing the type of leader that I am. Through speaking with knowledgeable people, mentors, and reading, I also developed those skills just through practice. By setting aside about an hour each week, generally on Fridays, to do some writing and thinking about how I want to continue with that shift. Just setting aside time was important."

SOFT SKILLS HAVE BIG UPSIDES

Most of the skills that these design leaders thought of as being paramount were also the skills hardest to measure, and may be the hardest to acquire as well. "Besides empathy?" says Jeb Banner. "Focus, for sure. Being able to tell you any minute of any day what are the things that matter most. Sometimes, I get off track, and part of it's because I'm starting new projects so often. So my mind is split between the nonprofits I'm involved with and the businesses I'm involved with and the ideas for things that are further down the pipe. I don't have a mind that naturally focuses, so I think I'm going to have to find a way to build more structure around my thinking and put more blinders on. Part of that is I'm committing this year to be more analog and to have less screen time, which I think leads to ADD thinking and behaviors." Changing behaviors, and acknowledging that they need to be changed, is a clear sign of leadership maturity. From our research into user experience, we also learned that behavioral change tends to be most effective when connected with accountability. This too was a sign of the more mature leaders we met with. "I need more accountability. I need to allow myself to be held accountable. I need to push my goals and commitments into a larger audience so that audience can come to me and say, 'Hey, you're way off track.'"

"I realized it a long time ago, but this week I just said to somebody yesterday, I'm actually making decisions and doing things that are going to affect about 15 people's lives this week—hiring, promoting, totally changing their lives," says Vince Lavecchia with a wide grin. "I don't really know how it happened. We just have been building on this idea of creating a great agency with great people. My job is to create a great company. Justin and JD, they make the work great. And so if I can find great people, and they can make the work great, we can continue to grow and live in a great environment. And we've just been doing that and chipping away at it and making decisions along the way.

Growing Companies by Growing Leaders

Leaders don't evolve in a vacuum. Their growth is connected to the groups they run. Instrument's Vince Lavecchia tells a familiar story about company growth and the personal challenges that it brings. As one grows, so does the other. "When we were four people, I was like, 'Man, what if we get to eight people?' And when we were 12 people, we were like, 'We'll never get to 40 people.' And when we were 40 people, we were like, 'Holy cow! This is huge. I don't know if we can even run a business bigger than 40 people.' We just didn't know. And then all of a sudden we were 80 people. And even then, I'm telling people, 'Look, I've never done this before—we're doing the best we can do,' and we're killing it. So yeah, it just has gotten there. But I really put it to the people that we found, the talent. Well, I think it has more to do with them than us."

"Oh, there's so many things," says Sarah Tesla with a wide smile when asked what else she still needs to learn on her path to becoming a design leader. "I think leadership is always a work in progress. I think that the more people that you become accountable to, the more you have to sort of, I don't know, push that drive, get people on board. What's the vision? Like, what are they getting behind? And, yeah, figuring out how to lead—that in itself is just a daily challenge. Am I being a leader by example, or am I sitting back too much on this one? It's always trying to find that fine balance." Knowing when to lean and when to lean back can be tough decisions for leaders. Finding the balance between the two is the magical land of perfection we all struggle to find. Tesla feels that her growth is also deeply connected to the choices she makes about who comes on board. She believes strongly that having the right balance of people in the studio says a lot about her leadership maturity and about her growth as a leader. "It's a fine balance of people. The team has been very carefully curated and, not to make that sound weird, but I'm just protective of that identity, I guess." Seeing their companies and teams as a reflection of their personal growth is a trait we noticed in several leaders. They see the world around them as a mirror to what's happening inside them.

These leaders are not leaders by accident. They all share a desire to lead. Their path to leadership might not always be direct or expected, but they all understand they now own that role. We wondered how they might advise themselves if they were given the chance. We were interested in how their experience might inform other leaders. With more knowledge, insight, and confidence, these current leaders can help younger or less experienced leaders make better choices. "I'm happy with my life now, so I wouldn't change too much," says SuperFriendly's Dan Mall. "But I would encourage some things that I did just to be a little bit stronger. I was always the weird employee that liked reading statements of work and operations manuals and things like that. I'd probably encourage myself to do more of that stuff. Without that stuff and having the bosses I had that encouraged me to do those things and were fine with it, I wouldn't be able to run a company. I was really fortunate to be able to learn from other people's mistakes and their failures. I like to observe those things and put them into practice. So I think I would suggest to my younger self, 'Do as much of that as you can and soak that up, because it's good training for running a company.'"

FINAL WORDS

As Sarah Testa pointed out, leadership is a work in progress. For leaders, their personal growth is not separate from the team's growth. Their advances reflect on the organization that they build and nurture. The organization they create in turn influences the growth of the people that work there. It's all connected. "That's my whole philosophy around it," says Steve Fitzgerald. "That's one of our values at Habanero. We're trying to build an organization that respects that dynamic in people's lives and allows them to create the professional sphere of that harmony in a way that respects other things that are happening in their lives." For these design leaders, there is a virtuous circle that connects their attitudes toward growth. The more they seek challenges that help them grow and learn, the more their teams do too.

KEY TAKEAWAYS

- If you are the leader, then your primary customer is your team.

- Having personal and professional purpose gives your growth strategies focus and clarity.

- Leaders invest in people and processes to keep distractions at bay.

- Surround yourself with advisors and mentors that provide insight into areas of growth.

- Most leaders need to constantly be developing their soft skills, like negotiation, presentation, and conflict resolution.

- Protect your personal and family time by communicating to your team when you're unavailable. Use your calendar to book this time before it's too late.

- Use design strategies to design an ideal life. Mapping out your days, weeks, months, and years gives you amazing amounts of control over your time.

- Exercise is the primary method for reducing stress and building reserves for a busy schedule. Walking, running, cycling, and yoga top the list of activities.

- Carving out time specifically to spend time with friends and family is considered by design leaders to be a critical part of a harmonious life.

- Work partnerships can be the source of harmony or stress. Find partners that complement your strengths and weaknesses so there's balance among you.

- Life comes in waves. Use the ebbs to recharge for the times when things will be busy.

Planning for the Future

Introduction

Designers, and especially digital designers, are often creating work on the cutting edge of technology. This can be both exciting and frustrating. Getting a grip on which technologies will survive the market's demands and which are just passing fads can feel like a daily investigation. As my 10-year-old son said when he was asked what career he wanted one day, "How can I know that? The things I'll be working on haven't even been invented yet." We live in a time where things change so fast that even the not-too-distant future can seem ambiguous. Knowing how to plan for a future that is unclear can be a design leader's most challenging strategic task. External forces aren't the only thing leaders need to concern themselves with; their entire company is also looking to the leader to show the way forward.

Given the ambiguity of the future, the act of planning can seem daunting to many design leaders. Seasoned designer and leader, Jules Pieri, CEO of Grommet, puts planning into perspective when she says, "Today in this business, it isn't as simple as, 'Oh, this is my planning week' or 'This is a planning meeting.' I have to step back at the beginning of every year and write what is called a CEO letter. I reflect on the top learnings from last year and the top goals of the coming year. That is probably the only formal time when I absolutely am thinking that way. But the rest of the year, it's about connecting the outside world to the one inside this business. As one of my investors said to me, 'Jules, your job is to be out there and absorb it. You've got to do that. Nobody else can.' That was actually kind of liberating … because [he said it during] a heavy operating phase…. [I]t gave me permission to do some things that I wouldn't do before. Design leaders might feel they don't have the time to do this, but it's their responsibility." Lifting your head out of the daily operations and focusing on the outside world is a requirement of leadership. As the saying goes, it's the leader's role to work *on* the business—not *in* the business.

I'm personally a big fan of planning in both my personal and professional life. For me, it's a process that evolved from simply writing a few annual resolutions to creating detailed plans for each aspect of my life. My favorite planning trick is to pretend I have to present my plan to a large audience of my peers. It forces me to think through the elements that might be questioned by others in similar positions to me. Preparing a keynote presentation for this fictitious audience seems to trick my brain into taking each goal or step more seriously. I've heard of other leaders who make their plans more visible by creating vision boards or timelines. These techniques might seem quaint until you realize these are exactly the same methods used to design products and websites. Mood boards, experience maps, user stories—they are all just formalized processes for visualizing and planning for an unknown future.

Natural Planners Versus Learned Planning

I wondered if our design leaders were natural planners or whether it was a skill they developed over time. My personal experience was that planning was a learned skill, but from observing my fellow studio owners in action, I discovered that some leaders come to this work more naturally. Either way, effective planning skills generally come with experience, and the extent of the planning that's required changes as the needs of the organization change. "I would not say I'm a great planner. I think it's something I'm becoming better at," says 352 Inc.'s founder Geoff Wilson. "I think historically our agency was lacking a little bit of vision because of the fact that we lived very day-to-day and didn't necessarily look long-term. Today, I do think planning is very important from both a strategic perspective as well as from a financial perspective, and it's something that I'm becoming better with and more disciplined about." Even well-established companies like 352 Inc. seem to learn the value of planning only when they reach a certain maturity.

In the case of whether to plan or not, size does seem to matter. Smaller companies worry less about long-term planning. It's just not that important to them. However, the growth of a studio or firm means new attitudes about planning are necessary. Success up until then can often be attributed to having really talented people, so a lack of planning doesn't affect their outcomes too much. I call this the "smart-lucky-strategy." A small group of smart and lucky people can get away without a strategy for some period of time—sometimes years. The problem comes when projects get more complex, the group grows, and communication becomes harder or good luck dries up. A growing organization demands a different approach.

Planning strategies vary among design leaders. "Am I a planner? Yes and no," says Sarah Tesla. "I plan ahead enough in order to feel confident about my next move and whether or not I would fail in that move. But beyond that, no. I like to have big ideas that would be interesting to reach, but I'm a little bit more of a 'live in the moment' kind of person than I am a meticulous planner." Everyone we spoke to approaches planning a little differently, but they all acknowledged that it is essential.

Even if you're not a live-in-the-moment type of person, Tesla's approach to crafting a big idea that's interesting to her is exactly where good planning starts. Regardless of the size of your group or organization, you'll need a clear vision of where you're headed—the clearer the vision, the better. Clear visions also need to engage your emotions. Big ideas create motivation and excitement for the team trying to reach them. Big ideas are worth getting out of bed and going to work for. Small ideas are easily forgotten. When we started Fresh Tilled Soil 10 years ago, we convinced ourselves we could be the first choice user-experience designers of all category leader clients. It was an insanely big goal for two guys in a basement without much experience in this space. We are a decade into our journey, and we hear weekly from our prospects and clients that we were indeed their first choice. In hindsight, our big, hairy, audacious goal doesn't seem so scary after all.

Reflecting on the need to adjust planning habits, Velir's Dave Valliere confirms that for him it's an evolving skillset. His approach to planning has gone from passive to proactive. "I would say that over the last few years, my desire to plan ahead has changed. When I first moved into my role in leadership, it was very reactive. I think we hit an inflection point as an organization. About 5 years ago, we were about 50 people. We didn't have a lot of organization, both in our own internal structure and how the staff are organized—literally any sort of organizational structure around our process for delivering to clients. We had a lot of issues with deployments to production that were causing outages for clients. Albeit they weren't huge outages, but they were noticeable." Valliere admits that sometimes it's the pain and frustration of a situation that forces the learning moment. Under the pressure of fast growth, the solutions to planning for a more stable future often require some quick experimentation. "During that time, I was very reactive to those situations. We were trying to plug holes. And sometimes when you're plugging those holes, you're only aware of what's right in front of you and not looking a little bit more broadly or a little bit over the horizon. It was hard to be more strategic and think about planning. We were growing a lot and we were adding a lot of new staff. We were onboarding a lot of new accounts. Figuring out an organization that scaled to support that while you're in some of those issues at the time is a little messy. You're trying things around an organizational structure. And I do remember a couple of instances where we tried something from an organizational management structure that just wasn't right and had to switch it around."

Valliere stepped back from the Band-Aid approach to planning and spent about a year thinking about what was going to have the biggest impact on Velir over the next 10 years. By spending a lot more time thinking about the steps that would get them there, he was able to gain control over their growing pains. He continues, "What will get us to that space? Do we really want to double-down as an implementation firm? Or do we want to expand into a more full-service agency where we're offering services that go beyond just pure development and implementation? These were the things I was thinking about." By asking the right questions, he was able to work with his executive team to find the answers. The next stage was planning the steps that would implement those answers. "This was important, both from the perspective of building a portfolio and getting the right staff involved and trained. So I would say from that perspective, we've been able to think more and plan more. For me, things have gotten more comfortable. I'm a lot more effective at thinking about what we want to be doing in terms of these new service areas, and then asking, '[W]hat are the steps that we can then step through over the next however-amount-of-time-it-will-take to try to get there?'"

"I think it's been a mix of both natural and learned skills," says Scott Baldwin of Yellow Pencil. "I've always been a 'zero inbox' kind of guy, just about. I'm pretty good at kind of trawling through ... my information. But I think a lot of it is just coming down to having a clear head and taking clear actions at the right times." Having a clear head means having the strategies to deal with everything from email to annual budgeting. Developing these strategies often comes from experimenting with what works for your style of leadership. Being in touch with your leadership style helps you choose the best planning methods. "We've taken an absolutely strategic approach to planning," says Jason Grigsby of CloudFour.

"A few years ago, we did a bunch of Strengthsfinder[1] exercises. These are the tools found in the Strengthsfinder books." By identifying what the executive team was good at, they were able to find solutions that best meshed with their strengths. "I don't think I can turn off that strategic part of my brain. According to the Strengthsfinder tools, I fall into the achiever, strategic, futuristic categories. I spend way, way too much of my time in thinking mode ... A lot of what we're doing is trying to figure out how we will get to where we want to go."

That Pesky Ambiguous Future

We also asked the design leaders what they see when they look at the industry as a whole. We wanted to know what they see coming down the line in the way of opportunities, challenges, and trends. Dominic Bortolussi of The Working Group sees a future where clients want more than just design and development services. "I think one thing that we're uncovering for ourselves is that as the size of our clients grows—they're getting bigger and bigger, national and international companies—we're realizing that they're looking for someone who provides more than just the production, more than just slapping design on a piece of software. They're looking for the smarts and the strategy in advance of that. We've always provided that, but we never focused on that until recently because our genesis was as a development shop."

As design teams grow and their skills go beyond pushing pixels, the desire to take on more strategic work increases. More strategic work means more internal planning. Delivering on complex projects requires teams with training in strategic thinking. "In the past, we were just the guys behind the scenes who'd be coding the apps," says Bortolussi. "As the size of our projects has grown, the need for that type of strategy has grown. That means that agencies like ours are going to need to be able to offer more and more of that type of work in concert with the development process. Using the agile process, which is something that we've adopted over the last three or four years, strategic thinking is very tightly intertwined with the production. Every cycle ... goes through a piece of strategic process and strategic thinking about what you want to develop and why you want to develop it and how to prioritize that."

The lesson here is that planning for successful outcomes at the project level also means flexing your planning muscles at the company level. The two are

---

1 Strengths Finder 2.0 by Tom Rath (*http://www.strengthsfinder.com/home.aspx*)

always connected. You can't deliver strategic value to your clients if you can't answer those questions for your own design organization. "Educating our clients into that process is going to lead to better things, better production, better software," continues Bortolussi. "I think that's a common theme that we've seen with a lot of our peer agencies around here. Rather than just being the design and dev shops, they're being asked their thoughts and expertise on how to design a [website] for a client based on their business needs."

Habanero Consulting has been in business for two decades, and CEO Steven Fitzgerald is planning for several more decades of business. With so many short-term-focused planning methodologies like Agile and Lean gaining popularity, you might mistakenly think that long-term planning was only for your dad's generation. You'd be wrong. Whether they actively plan for the future or not, all our design leaders think about what the long-term future will mean for their teams and opportunities. Planning far ahead can seem daunting, but that far-away future appears to excite our design leaders. "That's what's fascinating and cool and, frankly, super inspiring for me," says Fitzgerald. "We're very detailed on measuring employee engagement and workplace health. Aside from some systems issues, one of the key areas for us to get better at and, as a company, to improve engagement in right now is clarity of vision. We've been on a three- or four-year journey to get clear about where our next step is and where we're going.... I said to the team, 'There's a change in the world that we feel we want to play a role in.' It's all related to our purpose around helping organizations and people thrive. My belief is that we need to create a long-term vision that says, 'These are our values, this is the opportunity in the market, this is where the world's going to spend their money...,' and then position ourselves—to poorly quote Wayne Gretzky—[to] skate to where the puck's going to be in terms of the market."

Planning for the future means picking a strategy that isn't going to fade with time. Hitching plans to trendy technologies or fashionable industries can often result in temporary success. To be able to deliver on a long-term plan, our design leaders always reference the core of why they are in business. Aligning their plans to the fundamentals is how they ensure a timeless strategy. "I think vision needs to come from thinking about why you exist, your purpose, [and] understanding how that will most successfully unfold over time," says Fitzgerald. "You need to think about the other market dynamics and the other realities of that. We want to drive our vision based on how we can best live our purpose over time. That gives me a different perspective to think about where we want to go as a company and the role we want to play in creating this bigger change. It's related to the impact we can have on our customers and their cultures, and helping their organizations thrive."

"For me, it's constantly learning," Greg Hoy says of thinking about the future and the surprising rewards it brings. "One of the absolute gifts that happened to me was starting Owner Camp.[2] One of the motivating factors was to create a potentially alternate revenue stream moving forward. I didn't anticipate that it would provide so much professional development opportunity for me. Talking to people like yourself who do what [you] do and learning from them, and learning what the life cycle of a leader might be. For me, I'm kind of in the awkward teenage years of running an agency. I've got braces and headgear and I'm still trying to figure out [whether I am] doing the right things. At the end of this, are we're going to blossom or are we going to have to retreat? You think about all those things. You think about what constantly energizes you moving forward."

Aligning Plans to Culture

The size, structure, and culture of your design team will often have a significant influence on the plans you create. Each group will be different, and it's the responsibility of the design leader to recognize what the organization can honestly support. Planning to do something just because everyone else is doing it is naive at best and disastrous at worst. Just like the individual strength-finding exercises, leaders need to ask what their organization excels at doing. This also means recognizing what their weaknesses are. For companies that have the culture or structures that support developing their own internal products, this can mean they are able to support plans for that. "One thing that I really want to get into as an agency, is to be able to develop our own products and start to have product revenue … to complement our service revenue," says Geoff Wilson. "This is scary for agencies. Usually you hear horror stories of this not working, but we're trying to be very, very disciplined about it. I think that's really important for our long-term survival. I think that to have a diversified stream of income, so it's not 100% client-services-focused, is where I want to see us get to."

"Our planning for the future is really about finding a way to keep the culture and grow the culture, because we think that the success of our future is predomi-

---

2 Owner Camp is a retreat held several times a year by the Bureau of Digital for owners and senior executives of design studios.

nantly [reliant] on our culture," says Funsize founder Armendariz. "Our business comes from word of mouth, so to date we've never invested any money in marketing or business development.[3] A lot of our business comes from the fact that people know we have a very good culture, and a lot of the cool things that we're doing come from the culture. In terms of how I see it, most of my planning is going to be involved in maintaining, grooming, and bettering our culture."

"I would say, fairly loose," Brian Williams says of their approach to connecting plans to any one technology or sector. "Our view is that change is inevitable. We're in an industry that's constantly changing. Stuff that works now won't work in two years, didn't work two years ago, that sort of thing. We're constantly seeing that, whether it's the tech stack that we're using [or] the process that we're using, the tools are always changing [and] the client's needs are changing. Since we sometimes work with startups, we have to be cautious of their ups and downs. Some of the startups are hot right now, but when that bubble bursts in a year or two, they'll be gone. So we can't be overly reliant on that."

Relying too much on one market sector or trend is dangerous. Flexibility with planning is always a balance between what's good for the organizational culture and what's good for the market. Greg Hoy confirms Williams' line of thinking, "You have to keep asking yourself, do client services still energize you moving forward? Does focusing on a particular niche energize you more than another? Can you construct an organization around you to keep you motivated so you are in that niche and constantly energized? I think about that stuff a lot. I'm not the guy to be designing sites and performing critiques and things like that, but I think I offer some experience in other areas that some newer people in our office don't have that I could potentially leverage into some new business opportunities for us. I'm always thinking about what's next and how I can add value to the organization, [and] we've kind of filled the stuff that I used to do with other very talented people."

Williams goes on to describe how they avoid the rollercoaster ride associated with tech trends and fashionable industries. "So we have built the entire structure around this bet on change. Our future planning is often saying, 'Well, what are we interested in doing in terms of the teams? What kind of technologies do we want to play with? When we look out two years from now, or five years from now, what types of clients do we want? What types of solutions are we trying to solve?' That sort of thing, but it's not very rigid. We're not trying to make an exact

---

3 Update: Funsize recently hired a head of business development.

plan for how to get there. We want to have a clear vision in terms of what we're trying to achieve, but we ... accept the fact that change is going to be constant." Connecting plans to a timeless vision works best for design organizations. Instead of choosing a trending technology, design leaders focus on the underlying reason that technology exists. For example, social media isn't the trend, it's the desire for humans to remain connected so they can share information. That basic human desire probably won't ever go away. A smart design leader sees that and gears their plans to leverage that in their choice of tactical investments.

This focus on the underlying principles of human behavior is not just limited to technology and industry verticals. Design leaders also recognize that foundational principles relate directly to how they lead, manage their people, and curate their cultures. "Some of this is the trendy management approaches we see and hear in the media," observes Williams. "You hear it all the time. One example is to fire people quickly. It's not meant in a callous way at all because it's not doing anybody any good to have the wrong person in the organization. I learned pretty quickly that I don't like that 'hire slow, fire fast' kind of thing. I think the idea of firing fast is a little too cold for our structure and culture. I think the idea of finding people who are unhappy and unsuccessful, and [figuring out] a way to get them out of the organization [and to a place] where they will be happy and successful is a good thing. I think that's important." Williams goes on to explain that when he needs to let someone go, he'll spend a lot of time finding the right place to send that person. Identifying job opportunities helps them leave with their head held high and without having to face the financial challenges of being unemployed. Williams believes that planning for those outcomes reinforces the culture of his company and ensures a more positive future for everyone on the team.

Planning for Success, and Not the Other Thing

In the absence of a plan, leaders will very often end up at the helm of a rudderless ship. Worse still is that someone else's plan might hijack the ship and set it on a path that has dire results. This hijacking happens subtly and often goes unnoticed until it's too late. It starts with something small like a request from a client to do a noncore project. A client suggests that the design firm adopt a new project that's out of their wheelhouse so that the client's needs can be addressed. Next thing you know, the design firm is hiring people they don't really need for a project they don't really want. The client isn't at fault. They just see a competent design partner suggesting they can respond to a request. Before long, the design leader finds herself running a business that's spread too thin and has no prospects for the services they currently offer. These distracting events aren't a problem if you're focused on what you stand for and how you'll get there. The problem is when you have no plan. So how then do successful design leaders plan for a positive outcome?

The first step appears to be getting the company plan aligned with what the firm can be really good at, and aligned with the reality of the market. Knowing your cultural strengths, understanding the market trends, and then connecting the dots is the best way to start. Steven Fitzgerald explains how they identified their sweet spot, "We're in a really interesting industry right now where in the long term we feel that technology, process, and culture in our organizations need to come together in different ways than they do right now," says Fitzgerald, "the product design industry uses technology in a way that's oriented around making processes easier. We know that there's massive opportunity for technology, process, and culture to play a role in changing how people relate to each other, how they relate to their organizations, how great their careers are, and the productivity those organizations get from those people."

Developing a strategy isn't just about filling a need. It's a careful study of what the restraints are for a solution to be created, and then determining which policies and guidelines will get the company to the point where they can deliver the solution to their clients. "It's not simply using technology to make something like a payroll process simpler or a supply chain simpler," Fitzgerald continues. "That's what technology is used for today, and it's very important, but it's using the combination of technology, process, and culture to shift the overall experience that people have. We need to change the experience that organizations have with their people, and change the whole dynamic so we create more thriving organizations." This big-picture thinking described by Fitzgerald elevates the planning out of the minutia of what tech to focus on and up to the level of creating transformative experiences that are timeless.

That's just the first step. The next step is figuring out how to communicate that transition to the market so they can see the value of these solutions. "We have to create a bit of a shift in the next five years," says Fitzgerald. "The question is, how do we get our market and our customers thinking about us more in terms of some of those bigger cultural changes? How do we become transformation agents?" These challenges do not only present themselves to larger design firms but are important for internal design groups and smaller consultancies to consider as well. User-experience and product designers are frequently lumped in with graphic designers and engineers. Crafting a strategy that differentiates solutions and illustrates relevant outcomes is the biggest challenge. "Our industry, and organizations like us, are typecast as technology companies or design organizations or agencies," Fitzgerald says. "It's tough to get out of that typecast, to get involved in the right conversations, to be involved in organizational change, to get into the meat of that. Yet we know that what we have to offer is critical to create those outcomes in the organizations we're dealing with, so we have to overcome that hurdle."

It's clear that in order to remain relevant, design leaders will need to focus less on individual technologies and more on product-wide or organizational solutions. Leaders will have to focus on not being known just as a technology-oriented or design-oriented consulting firm but one that is associated with very specific business outcomes. It could be experiential or cultural change, but it can't just be about technology. "I think [we made mistakes] around being too broad on our tech stack, for example," says Williams. "We realized pretty quickly that trying to be a technologist that could work in any tech stack really just meant that we weren't very good at anything. It's easy to sell that way but not necessarily the way to do our best work, so narrowing in and being more specialized has been good."

Connecting the Dots

It might seem obvious that plans should have some return for the organization, but it's worth understanding how that happens. Returns take many forms and may not always be financial. Nonfinancial plans tend to be long-term in nature and thus can be more complicated to address when short-term needs, like cash flow, are on the organization's mind. For design leaders to create continuity between planning and returns, there has to be a link to what the plans will mean for the people in the organization. If the team can't see the returns that will result from the design leader's plans, they will be less motivated to make the behavior changes required to reach the planned goals. This is why the difficulty in measuring the returns on cultural and brand-specific plans makes them easy to ignore. The link between finance and nontangible outcomes is sometimes hard to describe, so it's essential that design leaders develop the communication tools to deliver this message clearly.

Communicating plans to the team consistently and effectively is a skill all design leaders need to have. Communicating a vision so that everybody else gets involved isn't just about presentations and motivation posters on the studio wall.

Sarah Tesla of Make describes the components of communicating a plan to the team when she says, "It should be a combination of two things. One is the vision of the business. This might not be something that you plan for formally, but it's important that everyone is on board with that vision. The second thing is beneath that. It's planning from a financial perspective, and certainly there's a bit more fiscal responsibility there. You can't ... be too reckless and say to the team, 'Oh well, money could run out and, you know, we'll just figure something out when we get there.' No, it's not like that. I've got more of my shit together in that space. And not that it's always perfect, but it's healthy enough that it doesn't feel too challenging." Tesla makes it clear that things are always changing. Even when plans are made, there should be an understanding that feedback will be received and adjustments are not far away. "If anything, you should plan for your vision to change and evolve. You have to be open to that, and not attached to things. I set the tone for what the vision might be, but ultimately I'm looking for cues from everyone on the team to ... give me an indication of what could be the best way forward."

"I live in the future," says Jules Pieri. "I don't think of it as a formal process. It's more about making connections. I have to expose myself to ideas and technologies regularly to do that ... So it means getting out of the office, it means reading, it means talking to people and applying discipline I learned early in my career as a designer. Nobody's paying me to design the past, or even the present, right?" Pieri is a consummate design leader and it's clear that she uses her design training in her everyday thinking. Researching first, then making connections to possible solutions is in her bones. "As CEO, I had to figure out how to get the information I needed to do that job. To me, that always meant hitting the road, figuratively and literally. Talking to customers, looking at competition, looking at the capabilities of my own company. Once I have the information, it's a sort of [a] blend of instinct and reaction to reality."

Vince Lavecchia of Instrument explains how they connect the dots on big, long-term projects like building a new office to house their 100-plus employees. These types of projects affect both financial and cultural outcomes. "We definitely look at the financial goals and say, 'Hey everyone, we're building a building.'" Lavecchia knows that having a creative workspace allows his team to generate better quality work so investing in a new office is essential. Office space, team size, reputation, and quality of work all mingle to create a reputation for the firm that keeps the work coming in. He's quick to point out how these things are intertwined. "We know we want to maintain a certain level of success and performance on the financial side, and that's going to allow us to keep reinvesting in the company. We just have to be responsible to those numbers, but once you set those goals, then it's just about having the discipline to force everybody to manage their projects and their teams to reach those goals. In that way, we are not financially focused because we firmly believe that if we do insanely good work, we're going to keep getting insane work, and people will naturally find out about us and see it and want our work. We create demand by putting out insane work. We keep the supply managed so that we're always in demand. We've been intentional about hiring size and not blowing up. We could definitely be larger if we wanted to maximize money, but we've intentionally been careful about that."

Connecting Plans to Specific Revenue Outcomes

Many of the design leaders we interviewed have routines around their planning processes. For some of the more seasoned leaders, these routines are deeply ingrained in their everyday activities. You might even say they are habits. Understanding that these habits or routines have the ability to bring plans to life is something design leaders talk about frequently. "I never, never, never slow down on the sales side even though we could be busy and we would have client work booked out for the next six months," says Brian Williams about the time he spends actively implementing his plans for the future. Williams' daily activities are seen through his lens of what will happen in the months ahead. "That might seem like forever and we might feel like there's no need to sell, but six months goes by very quickly and all of a sudden we might have nothing in the pipeline. Always be selling is a big thing." William's insistence on thinking about selling means he's constantly planning for positive sales outcomes. This is a good reminder that planning isn't always an annualized event but a daily habit that can be reinforced through ritual and routine. Making the time for daily reflection and connecting big-picture goals to daily activities is another thing that makes these design leaders successful.

Allotting time to planning new initiatives and integrating them with daily activities doesn't happen by accident. Geoff Wilson describes how they plan to take ideas that the team has and deliberately turn them into products that can generate new revenue. "We ask each team to think of at least one product idea that they as a team would get behind and would like to bring to market. We get all of our teams together and they think of ideas. We go over the ideas with them over the course of a few months and then we solidify the idea that each team is going to pursue." What Wilson does next is an example of thoughtful planning.

"Once we have these ideas, we give each of our teams three days. We take three days off of client work, shut the whole entire agency down ... and we do a hacka-thon, company-wide." This focused time allows his teams to get the work done without distractions. Instead of giving them something superficial, suggesting 20% of their time toward these projects, Wilson dedicates the entire company's resources to the project. This planning gets the best results in the shortest amount of time.

Planning these high-impact projects this way has significant time advan-tages, but it's the entire experience that Wilson is excited about. Not only is his team building something of value but they are reinforcing positive team dynam-ics and bonding culturally with one another. "It's a tremendous event [and] a lot of fun. Everyone gets really into it. People stay up late all three nights. Both years we've done it, we've had at least one team stay up all night.... At the end of the three days, they have to a do a business pitch where they have to pitch the con-cept for their business product. This is similar to how they might pitch a venture capitalist for investment. They have to pitch the concept of their product and they have to demo their product, whatever they were able to get accomplished in the three days. They do a live demo for us and they do this to a panel of judges. We bring in external judges to help us judge it. This year, [we brought in] Dan Mall from SuperFriendly and Andi Graham, owner of Big Sea. We had six judges in total and they helped us judge the different projects and pick the winner. We give the winning team two months off of client work to build an MVP[4] of their prod-uct to allow us to actually bring their product to market, and if the product pro-duces any revenue for the company in the future, we share a percentage of [it] with the team."

Sales and spin-off products aren't the only way to plan for positive bottom-line results. Packaging knowledge or services can be just as effective in planning for new revenue streams. Several years ago, we launched an apprentice program that quickly became a source for new talent at Fresh Tilled Soil. Within a few semesters, the program was generating hundreds of thousands of dollars in reve-nue. Our experience wasn't unique. Other design leaders have used their indus-try knowledge to build teaching and apprenticeship programs. Jason VanLue's Envy Labs turned their online design skills platform, Code School, into a million-dollar business that eventually sold to Pluralsight for $36 million. "Right now I'm very, very passionate about teaching," says Dan Mall. "I find I get the most

---

4 MVP: Minimum Viable Product

fulfillment out of that. And SuperFriendly is a small company. It's one person, one employee. I have no plans to grow larger than one employee, but the thing that I'm doing right now is I run an apprenticeship program. I do a nine-month apprenticeship with people that have an appreciation for design and development but don't know anything about it. My goal is to get them from zero to sixty in nine months. The future for me, if all goes well, is to run a full-time apprenticeship and maybe another business. SuperFriendly the agency, the collaborative, is its own business. SuperFriendly the apprenticeship, or SuperFriendly the academy or whatever, becomes its own business as well." These planned-for outcomes have a double or even triple bottom line because they add value to the organizational culture, improve revenues, and lift the community as a whole.

Be Bolder and Wiser

In the interviews with the design leaders, we asked what advice they would give to a younger version of themselves. "I thought about that recently because I spent a lot of time wandering in my twenties, playing music and working odd jobs and not really getting my shit together," says Smallbox CEO Jeb Banner. "It wasn't until I met my future wife that things started to click in a lot of ways. To my younger self, I'd say, 'Enjoy the chaos and forget the bad times more. Enjoy the openness,' and probably mostly, I'd say, 'Don't be ashamed. Don't be shy. Don't be afraid to put yourself out there. Be bolder.'"

Some suggestions for planning in ambiguous times are more practical. If you're a new design firm like Funsize you might not have the experience and history for your banking partners to support you in times of need. In those moments the best advice is to treat cash as king. "Well, the first thing that we did," says Anthony Armendariz, "is get the AmEx card and get the line of credit. We'd talk to other design companies and we'd came back and say, 'Okay, let's get the line of credit.' We were so new that we hadn't filed our first year of taxes so we couldn't get the line of credit. What can we do? Well, we pretty much always had three to six months of cash in the bank, to make sure that if for some reason we lost all of our business today, we could cover payroll for six months. We don't necessarily like being that cash heavy, but that's provided us with the ability to not freak out about things like that." Being financially literate and conserving cash flow isn't just being practical; it's a requirement of keeping a business in the black. Getting the right guidance on fundamentals like this separate, healthy design businesses from those that barely survive month to month.

Nothing escapes reality. Even big, hairy, audacious goals need a roadmap to get them to their destination. Planning for a better future means getting practical. Big goals need big plans. "I plan to change the way businesses work," says Banner of his long-term goals. "I feel very strongly that the workplace is fucked up. Someone mentioned at a conference that 20% of employees are engaged by their work, and that, to me, that is the big opportunity. If we want to build really meaningful brand experiences, it starts with the employee or creator experience. Everything I'm doing right now is moving toward, 'how can we build a more meaningful employee experience for us, as well as the sister companies and our clients?' These plans are not there yet on a thought leadership level, so I want to push myself into that realm as a thought leader. I need to do more writing. I plan to write a book this year. I'm taking a month off in July to do some introspection and writing. I'm sketching out ideas right now, and I'm open to it being whatever it becomes."

Staying Relevant

Whether design leaders make big plans or small plans, they all need to connect to what the market needs are at that point in time. With the constantly shifting technologies, methodologies, and skills needed to deliver value, possibly the biggest challenge is remaining relevant to clients. "At a very high level, I think staying relevant is the biggest challenge," says Armendariz. "This was the core topic of the presentation that I gave at a conference recently. If you look at history, in our early days of designing digital products, we had a bit of a mish-mash of different skills. Because of interactive authoring tools and animation tools, we knew a little bit about motion graphics, we knew a little bit about sound and audio, we knew a little bit about interaction design, visual design, and we used all these tools ... and canvases that we worked in. Then as the web got more mature and as iOS was released, our skills got a little bit narrow. We developed these very narrow skillsets. Now if you look at the way that technology is going, not just in the user interfaces themselves but all the different kinds of digital products that are out there, if we don't stay sharp across a wide range of skillsets, I think we could very easily see ourselves being irrelevant. It happens so fast that it might not necessarily be three years from now, but maybe even a year from now."

Focusing in on one or two areas seems counterintuitive but it's the only way to keep ahead of the shifting landscape. You can't make everyone happy by spreading yourself too thin across dozens of domains. Being relevant to everyone means you're no longer relevant. "In our shop, we only do design, so this might make more sense when I say this. We've learned very quickly we can't just get away with delivering flat PSDs [Photoshop documents] and wireframes and prototypes anymore. If we can't figure out how to bridge that gap between design and technology, and speak the same language that an engineer is speaking and working in their environment, which honestly is the canvas—Photoshop isn't the canvas, the technology is—then we're going to be irrelevant. I've already seen a lot of other design shops struggling with that. I think we need to put a lot of planning for the future into that area. We need to always be building new skills in that area."

FINAL WORDS

Planning isn't a solitary exercise. Design leaders can't be expected to take on the challenges of the future without help. The best plans happen when the design leaders get input from their team, their advisors, and their partners. Our interviews confirmed that the most successful design leaders rely on outside input. "I honestly don't think that I would be able to do what we do without my partners," says Devbridge Group cofounder Aurimas Adomavicius. "When we founded the company, there were five of us. Now, we've grown to eight partners in the business. I really don't think we would be who we are if it were just myself alone or the original founding three. It's also been incredibly important for us to bring in partners as we grow who are much more sophisticated in specific areas than we are. We started this business without really having done this before.... We knew tech, we knew design, but we didn't know how to build a business. As we scaled and as we brought in partners, we looked for people who were phenomenal in their areas or known in the community for engineering. Then we brought in a person who did product ownership at Rolls Royce." Adomavicius explains that as his team grew, he actively planned to hire people with specific skills to get the business to its destination. "As you assemble that team, you can bring in these players that will essentially lift the organization to a different level when they join the company. Then we formed the functional board out of the shareholders in the organization. We're considering now also creating an outside advisory board where we can bring in some other people that we've established relationships with over the course of growing this business,... either partners in some of the ventures we're in, or just people that we really respect and we're friends with, who can potentially help guide us in the future."

KEY TAKEAWAYS

- Great plans first require a clear vision, guiding principles, values, and action steps.

- Creating plans allows you to focus the business activities and avoid distractions.

- Planning is a team sport. Get help from partners, advisors, mentors, and team members.

- The future is ambiguous so plans never survive intact. Make plans that are flexible enough to adjust to an ever-changing future.

- Planning for the future is often about finding a way to keep a culture that works.

- Big goals are worth getting up for but can only be achieved when you have clear plans.

- Companies and teams don't grow linearly. Plan for spurts of fast growth with slow periods in between.

- Long-term planning is not fashionable, but it's still the best approach to return value to the company and the team.

Leadership Styles

Introduction

Thankfully we're all different, and as we learned in Chapter 1, that diversity makes organizations stronger. No one will deny that different perspectives bring a healthy variety of ideas to the table. But the question remains: are there some styles of leadership that just work better than others?

Our interviews aimed to identify styles of leadership that produced positive results. We asked our design leaders about their leadership styles. We also asked them about the results those styles create, and then investigated whether their teams agreed with those approaches. By contrasting these perspectives, we were able to see which styles are most successful.

Failure as a Gift

"From a leadership perspective, I look at most of what I do as failure," says Bryan Zmijewski of Zurb. "I'm constantly failing. I like to use Babe Ruth as an example. Babe Ruth was an exceptional baseball player. He hit tons of home runs, but he also struck out as much as he hit home runs. Somehow he had a batting average of 300, which means to be one of the best baseball players in the world hitting, he was missing most of the time." It might feel counterintuitive to consider failure as a leadership style, but Zmijewski does just that. By opening himself up to the growth mindset and embracing moments of failure as learning opportunities, he's putting himself ahead of the game. "I think from a leadership perspective, we have these expectations that you're supposed to get right answers all the time, and that leadership has the right answers, when really we're trying to guide people through the result, whether it's good or bad. To get to the next place, what I am doing on a daily basis is making adjustments and corrections based on the feedback, and incorporating [that] back into our work and seeing where we can go with it. It literally is everything we do."

Releasing the desire to be right all the time seems to be something that many of our leaders struggle with. It's not the desire to be right but the fear that they might be wrong that drives this feeling. "I started the company really young," says Peter Kang of Barrel in New York. "I was 23 [and] my partner was 21, so we didn't know better about a lot of things in terms of working with each other and with our first employees. We were scared. That's the best way to put it because we operated a lot from a place of fear." Acknowledging that fear was getting in the way was the beginning of personal growth for Kang. Pretending to have all the answers was putting Kang and his partner into situations where they felt they needed to always be managing every detail of the business. This micromanagement is exhausting. Once they realized this wasn't working and accepted that they had to get familiar with failure, Kang and his partner got to a place of understanding. "In the beginning we were thinking that we're paying these people to do work for us and we weren't even sure we could trust that they were doing it. It's an awful mentality. Over the years, you understand that the best work comes when people feel like they have the room to grow and they're [supported], and there's an environment where they're not being micromanaged."

Kang goes on to describe how his leadership style has evolved since those early days. "There's no looking over their shoulders now because we trust that they're going to do their best work. Understanding that took a long time…. I got comfortable with the idea that things can happen even when I'm nowhere near because I know that I helped to create that environment." This idea of creating a safe place for others to be their best creative selves is not unique to Kang and Barrel. Dozens of successful design firms see this as their primary goal and align their leadership styles to encourage and reinforce that ethos. This frees the design leader of the need to control every aspect of the business. Instead, they create a trusting environment so their team can get on with what they are good at, and leaders like Kang can focus on more strategic issues. "That feels like a great personal achievement. For so long, I always thought I had to have a hand in it or I had to be the controlling factor."

"I think I learned it from my grandfather," remembers Matt Bertulli, CEO of Demac Media in Toronto, about how he learned to lead without feeling like he needed to know everything. "Our family had a large home decor design business in northern Ontario and I grew up in that business. We didn't have babysitters or daycare or any of that stuff. I basically grew up in the backroom of that office. I got to see my grandfather, grandmother, parents, and brothers all working for the family business. We all grew up in a very social environment with customers coming in all the time and going up to strangers' homes." No stranger to the failures that challenge all businesses, Bertulli, whose business is in its sixth year, still wonders how his grandparents and parents pulled it off successfully. "I say to my mom all the time, 'I don't know how you did this.'" Being in a growth mindset means you make peace with the fact that you'll make mistakes and that's okay. "My grandmother still just shrugs it off. She's like, 'You're never going to know what the hell you're doing.'" These off-the-cuff gems are more important than we might think. Believing that there is some magical way to avoid failure sets leaders up for heartbreak. Having a healthy mindset for growth means embracing failures and seeing the challenges as part of the path to something better. "I guess leadership for me is a funny word," adds Bertulli. "I think of it just in terms of daily actions, whereas others might think you're the leader by a certain title or responsibility. But there's not much difference."

The learning mindset was common in the leaders we interviewed. Seventy-five percent of our design leaders claimed that they are flexible and growth-minded. A further 25% described themselves as "super adaptable" or "chameleons." It is possible that the nature of our investigation also attracted those leaders who were most open to growing and learning. If that was the case, we were fortunate that we discovered so many lifelong learners—but possibly less fortunate to have a perspective on what static-mindset leaders do in the face of failure. In our view, leaders who don't react well to failure are probably not very good leaders. In a healthy mind, the flipside of failure is learning, so it's not surprising to find great design leaders become mentors or role models to others. Also not surprising is to find that growth-minded leaders also like to teach. Almost all the design leaders we interviewed write frequently, speak at conferences, and mentor other designers.

"My style is kind of a teacher style," says Dave Gray of XPLANE. "I'm a pretty hands-off teacher. I like to create structures in which people can learn and figure things out." This point is extremely useful. It's hard for design leaders to be present at every point of failure and provide insightful teaching when it happens. A significantly more effective approach is to craft an environment that supports learning when the teacher can't be around. Doing this involves several strategies but almost always incorporates the lead-by-example method. "My strength as a leader is to inspire and encourage people. I try to set an example in the work that I do that makes people look at me and say, 'Yeah, I want to be like that. I want to do that kind of stuff. I want to be that kind of person.' So I'm not only teaching; I'm also doing." I'm a big fan of this approach. As a leader, it's often difficult to not jump in to solve every problem that arises. Thinking of yourself as a teacher gives you permission to teach and then step back. Let failure happen from time to time to let the student grasp the lesson.

Being a practical example also has its challenges. Always doing and never delegating undermines any opportunity for the team to learn from their own experiences, and can feel a little like mistrust. "I try not to meddle in other people's work," says Gray. "Because I tend to be more critical, I try to compensate for that. I'm very critical of my own work. I'm kind of a perfectionist, so when I'm looking at other people's work, I try to mitigate that. I don't mitigate it by not talking about the things that I have criticisms about, usually. But I mitigate them by also saying all the things that I like, which is easy to forget. I don't usually tell those things to myself." Failure is your friend but that doesn't give leaders the right to only focus on negatives. Finding a balance in all things is the lesson here. Design requires critique, but it doesn't have to all be negative. Seek the positive and reinforce the positive lessons, not just the failures.

LEADING BY CONNECTING

Modern organizations have a lot of gray areas. One of those ambiguous areas is in how leaders create connections between themselves and their team members. "I'm a very casual person. I like being friends with the people that I work with," says Skottie O'Mahony of BancVue. "I kind of consider them my family. I'm very passionate about my team. I'm very protective of my team, and I'm very transparent." It's been said that having friendships with your employees or staff isn't a good leadership strategy. We can't say for certain if this is true. What we observed is that many of our design leaders have close friendships with the people they work with. This was not a universal characteristic, but rather one frequently observed in our visits to the design leader's offices. These friendships seem to come from the leader's interest and compassion for the people they work with every day. Rather than the traditional arms-length boss-employee relationship, these leaders showed a genuine interest in their employees' lives, both in and outside of the workplace.

"They know everything there is to know about me," says O'Mahony. To help his team get to know him and set up a reciprocal exchange of personal insights, O'Mahony opened up to his team in a nontraditional way. "Here at BancVue, I did a presentation just about me. I explained my background and how I got [here], where my inspiration comes from, stuff like that. Now I'm asking each team member to do the same thing. I've asked them to share with the rest of the team what their background is [and] what makes them tick, because I think that's really important for the rest of the people on the team and it will help the team." This idea is not unique. Getting-to-know-you-styled presentations were common in successful teams and almost always initiated from the top. For companies with remote teams, like nGen Works, their solution was to use Skype for sharing personal stories. Employees presented to the whole team on topics that were personally interesting and meaningful to them. Several design companies used tools like Know Your Company to allow new employees to share their backgrounds, interests, and experiences with the team. At Fresh Tilled Soil, we use a combination of tools like Know Your Company and company-wide meetings where people can share things that they want to share about themselves, including their interests.

It follows that when design leaders are open and transparent about themselves, their team members will often do the same. Getting on the same level as everyone else doesn't mean you relinquish your leadership status. "In some ways you have to view yourself as a peer. I'm just one of the folks in the group," explains Brian Williams. "It's not so much that everyone is a friend first but it's certainly a family friendly type of an environment. We aren't a family, we're a business, so it's an important distinction. My brother's my business partner and our sister heads up recruiting, so there's some family aspects to it, but I don't like the family business label because I think it gives people the impression we're not as ambitious as we are. We're no 'Mom and Pop.'" Williams' distinction is spot on. You can treat your business team as a family without having the traditional "family business" label.

For companies like Viget, it's nothing more than treating people with respect and taking care of them when they need your support. When speaking to Williams, it's obvious that he cares about his work family at Viget. "I think that comes through in my leadership style. I'm very involved with our people. I want to have a relationship with everybody in the company." For a reasonably larger agency like Viget—they have 70+ employees—it might seem surprising that Williams takes the time to conduct all the one-on-one interviews with his staff. Williams uses this time investment in his people to make a clear distinction between leadership style and management style. "I get flack from my peers about how I still participate in every annual review or one-on-one. I view this time as a way to keep a pulse on not only the company but the industry. I learn a ton in all those meetings. I'm just in awe of the people who I get to work with. It's a chance to sit down for 30 minutes and talk to them about how they're doing, what they are seeing, and what they are excited about. That's not management. It's a fascinating leadership conversation for me. I don't view that as a burden at all."

The reverse works, too. The annual reviews allow the team to learn from Williams and to get to know his style of leadership. They also get to tell him what works and what he could be working harder on. In what looks like a 360-style review, William's solicits feedback on his leadership and uses that feedback to grow and improve. "I think the feedback is probably a little bit too much in the weeds right now, but it's good feedback nevertheless," says Williams, who feels that these conversations are what give him the insights he needs to craft the best possible leadership approach for his company. He also acknowledges that there are other ways to open the conversation about leadership style to something more long-term focused. "To look further ahead, I go to conferences and meet with other CEOs and advisors." Meeting with other leaders and listening to how they approach their business challenges every day gives Williams the added insight he needs to craft a leadership style that is appropriate for the time but also evolving.

Connecting strategic leadership with outcomes that are greater than just the bottom line was a theme we heard again and again. Whether it's thinking of the company as a big family or building a community of successful people, the desire to create a lasting legacy was part of almost all the design leader's style. "I actually would like to be remembered for creating a supportive and creative community," says Karen Denby Smith, Partner and cofounder of the Boston-based Kore Group, "actually even more than for the quality of our work. Even more important than quality is the respect of individuals and people that we work with. I would rather it go down in history that Kore was a company that really cared about people and respected relationships." Business has changed significantly in the last few decades. It seems entirely foreign to me that we used to live in a world where companies prioritized revenues and profits over their people and clients. Maybe I'm naive and things haven't changed that much, but I can say for certain that people are at the center of great design leadership. Treating people with respect is the first step to creating a great design organization.

BALANCING HARD AND SOFT APPROACHES

This eagerness to develop cultures of triple-bottom-line returns shouldn't be mistaken for some hippy philosophy. The leaders we met with are very accessible when their team needs them, but tough when things get messy. "I'm very casual but intense when intensity is needed," says Tracey Halvorsen of FastSpot. "I think everyone knows they can have a beer with me. We can chit-chat. But I do think that leaders have to be willing to make tough decisions quickly when they're needed. Otherwise, you can do a lot of damage." Halvorsen goes on to explain the difference between being "hands-on tough" and micromanagement. "When I need to make hard choices with the team, I am not micromanaging. I love building a team where everyone has a lot of freedom, but the team can only do great work when they respect that culture, and that culture supports them." This last point reaffirms something we observed in all the successful design groups; they are run like businesses that use design as a method to deliver solutions. They are not designers who just accidentally find themselves in business. These leaders are characterized by a leadership style that is caring and kind but equally as focused on delivering value and keeping the business financially healthy. Leaders walk the tightrope of being nurturing and being tough. Successful design leaders hold these counterintuitive styles in their heads at all times and know when to deliver a hug and when to deliver a rebuke.

Knowing when to be a hard-ass and when to be a puppy dog isn't straightforward. Design demands attention to detail. While design leaders are often open, trusting, and empathetic, they can be equally as stubborn and steely when it comes to their craft. They obsess about details and get frustrated when others don't understand the language of design. Many of our design leaders seemed to be seeking a balance between design's myopic craftsmanship and a growth-minded openness that invites in new disruptive ideas. "There is a lot of transparency in what we do," says Karen Denby Smith. "But the other part of what we do is to look for people who have a very strong foundation in the pure philosophy of design. So if you don't understand the hierarchies of typography and color theory, you're not going to cut it at Kore Group." Finding a balance between the hard and soft skills of design is the challenge of good leadership. Knowing when to let go of the craftsman-like details and focus on the bigger picture of running a design business is an important characteristic of successful leadership styles.

Leaders reminded us frequently of the contract of trust between the design company and the people that work there. "I think it's lead with the heart," says Vince LeVecchia, Partner and General Manager at Instrument in Portland. "It sounds really cheesy, but for me I just want to connect with people and have an understanding. I'm sort of the people person. So if I can connect with people and have a sense of trust with them, then there's this bargain. They're coming here eight hours a day. I'm paying them for that. But there's more to it. We're giving plenty, so if I can keep that bargain on the trust level, we'll get a lot back." Being clear that they are in a business environment that requires an exchange of services and money doesn't obscure leaders like LeVecchia from the fact that there still needs to be trust between employer and employee. "My leadership style is to make sure that that's in balance all the time. If I can pass the straight-face test with every employee here, and have that connection with them, then I feel like I'm doing the right thing." This resonated with what we heard from other leaders like Brian Williams from Viget and Tracey Halvorsen from FastSpot. Strong personal connections lead to trusting relationships and that's good for business. It appears that this isn't just LeVecchia's lip service either. "Vin's the heart and soul of the company," says Justin Lewis, CEO of Instrument and LeVecchia's business partner.

These leaders invest time in getting to know who's on their team and what makes them tick. Integral to that is being available to everyone. "I think the biggest thing is I'm very approachable," says Skottie O'Mahony of BancVue. "I make sure that I meet with my team casually ... go out and have coffee or drinks or just walk around. We have a lake right by us so we walk around the lake just to get to know people ... so that they feel comfortable talking to me. I don't see myself as, you know, someone who's a hardcore manager—'You must do this. You must do that.' It's more that I'm the person that's there to remove the blocks. I'm the person to help them in their career." Leaders who see their primary role as making others successful tend to get the rewards they seek. Put another way, making sure the team can achieve their goals is the leader's single biggest contribution to the team. O'Mahony reminds us of the balance between soft and hard styles. "Apart from being approachable, I can be irreverent and very vocal. I speak my mind," says O'Mahony. "Ultimately, I'm very deliberate in what I do, and for the most part, I'm just there for my team. I think that's what they would say, too."

Sometimes the trust comes first and the structured approach comes afterward. "My leadership style has definitely changed over time," says Marcelino Alvarez, CEO of Uncorked Studios. "Early on, it was very much trust that everyone will do what they need to do. I think when you're five or six people, it's really easy to trust and not have to be hands-on on certain things." Small groups are inherently easier to manage because you're often sitting in the same space. "We're 22 people now, plus we have five or six freelancers and interns, so we're getting close to 30," reflects Alvarez. "So relying only on trust,... doesn't work. Conversations don't scale regardless of whatever technology tools you're using to stay in touch. It's forced me to look at what my management style is and realize that I've got a core team that I do trust. They're incredibly capable at their jobs.

But if we're not having frequent conversations about what it is that we should be doing and why, then that doesn't magically clone itself and get distributed to everybody."

This is something I have learned to balance myself. While it's natural for me to trust people and expect they will always do the right thing, it's not a guarantee they'll do their job. As our company grows, it becomes increasingly difficult to make certain that everyone knows what's expected of them. I find myself having to make the time to explain what my expectations are to each person in the company. One the one hand it's a fairly large investment of time, but on the other hand the results are very tangible.

Creating trust can only happen when you're authentic. That means being transparent about who you are and what's important to you. Successful design leadership often requires making hard choices about your own path. Being yourself often signals something stronger than your title. You don't have to be the CEO to lead and influence others. Your leadership style might not look like the traditional person in charge, but if it's real, it'll get the respect of the people around you. That respect creates trust. "I'm not going to ever be Jack Welch at GE or the CEO at a Fortune 500 company," says Jeff Kushmerek, who leads product design at Virgin Pulse. "But I know right now what I love doing. That means being myself, working with small teams, and throwing in '30 Rock' and 'Big Lebowski' quotes all day. That probably won't get me into the board room at some of these larger companies, but I need to be honest with myself." Kushmerek's honesty and openness with his team gives him the soft power he needs to get the job done.

The Long-Term Style

"Patient," says Steven Fitzgerald from Vancouver-based Habanero Consulting Group when asked about his leadership style. "I've realized over time that I'm very oriented around thinking about things in the long term. We didn't want to create a lifestyle organization." In an era where companies are thinking about multiple bottom lines and how they can "make a dent in the Universe," it's apparent that design leadership also needs a bigger goal than just a paycheck or an award. "There's nothing wrong with that. I'm not trying to portray lifestyle businesses as a negative thing, but we feel that there's a change to be made in the world that Habanero can play an important role in. It's not going to happen in 10 or 20 years. It's going to happen in the longer term. Unfortunately, I won't be suitable for this role for that period of time."

Fitzgerald's attitude is common among successful service design leaders. Unlike product companies that have a clear path to an exit, service companies tend to be in it for the long term. Acquisitions and IPOs are a rare outcome for service businesses. This gives their leadership fewer options and, counterintuitively, more focus on strategies to deliver long-term value to their clients. "There's going to be a lot of turnover and change and evolution and growth. We need to build an organization that will last a really long time," says Fitzgerald. "We put a lot of thought into organizational sustainability. I always think that you're building an edifice for people to come and practice in your culture and share your ideas." He uses the metaphor to make his point. Fitzgerald imagines he's creating a building with really thick walls with a high point that reaches up to the sky. "It would be a beautiful place for people to come and share ideas. We're trying to build this organization in that way, not with any religious context but to make really thick, deep foundations, which is why we invest so heavily in things like hiring … and culture. We're much more concerned about how things are unfolding in the long term and where we have to go. We have this sense of purpose and change we want to create in the world. We know it's going to take a long time. I think that requires a lot of patience."

Thinking long term is hard—especially for young leaders who may be reacting to peer pressure to get big fast. "The older we get, the more patience we learn, and I think it's done me personally a world of good," says Karim Marucchi of Crowd Favorite. "The younger you are, the more you want to go out there and attack, and get that client, and get that project out there." Marucchi has had the benefit of working in several organizations, both big and small, and knows the value of patience. "You learn when you can say no, and when you can pass up a certain opportunity because you can find another one. You just learn how to deal with different points of stress better." Marucchi has learned this lesson the hard way. Having personally stewarded 43 mergers and acquisitions in the agency space, he's well aware that patience is key to success. "In my career, I've made deals that were made purely for the immediate bottom line, and there were deals that were made with the long-term value in mind. I prefer the latter."

LOTS OF STYLES, ONE GOAL

No two design leaders we interviewed were the same. Their backgrounds, experiences, skills, genders, and cultural diversities made finding commonalities in styles difficult. In spite of this, they all seemed to be striving for a singular common outcome: make their teams successful. "I think for me, my management style, it's always in flux," says Marcelino Alvarez of Uncorked Studios. "To be honest, I'm learning from the size changes that we've gone through. I've changed my one-on-one policy. I would do one-on-ones with my direct reports [at a frequency that] for me felt like it was often enough, every four weeks, maybe five, maybe six. And now I'm doing weekly one-on-ones. I've been doing that for about a month and that was a big change. I was talking to another CEO friend of mine here in town. He told me 'We do all the one-on-ones. We just schedule it all the same day.' Whereas before I was scheduling my one-on-ones over a rolling six- or seven-day period, now I do 25-minute one-on-ones ... every Thursday. From a schedule perspective, it feels like I'm giving up an entire day every week but that's not what it actually feels like on the other side of doing these meetings. If you're having eight conversations all on the same day, you're aware of incidents and can respond to things in real-time." Having such close contact with his team gives Alvarez the opportunity to help his team in immediate terms. Not having to wait for annual check-ins or reviews gives his team the opportunity to learn, teach, and grow in ways that other organizations can only dream of.

For design leaders like Dan Mall at SuperFriendly in Philadelphia, their leadership style fits into the operational model they have created. SuperFriendly uses the Hollywood model of team management to pull together ad hoc design teams for specific projects. Delivering on great work when you have a new team for every project requires nerves of steel. So it seems appropriate that collecting talent for a time-boxed outcome is the job of a director. "For the projects that I pull together, I'm the director," says Mall of his role and leadership style. "I think that this [Hollywood] model scales really well in that I can create as many teams as I want to. The reason that I don't have 100 teams running at once is that when I stretch myself too thin, it affects my directing ability. So I try to limit the amount of projects that I'm working on to only the things that I can be directly involved in. That way, I can keep my focus on those projects. Knowing that the common thread in all SuperFriendly projects is me, I need to uphold the quality of all of those projects. If I can't deliver that, then I'm not really going to have a good portfolio of work. I'm not going to be able to sell that work. So since I have to be that thread, I try to hold that thing to be as consistent as possible."

Directing projects requires both tactical and strategic leadership. Being clear about the outcomes of the project can't be achieved by holding your tongue. "I'm pretty direct on the stuff that I like to do and the visions that I have for projects," says Mall. "I'm not shy in making those things known, but I try to leave as much openness for the person that I'm hiring to bring their thing to the table, or their skill to the table. I [see] my job as more of a curator,... how can I find the people that are doing the best work? And how can I create enough space for them to do that work uninhibited? So some people want to be involved in the business side, some people just want to come in to Photoshop, and for both of those people my work is to help them do their jobs more effectively." Whether you choose to see yourself as the director on the set of a movie, like Mall, or the spiritual leader of your team, like LeVecchia, it's essential to communicate exactly what you want from your team. Clear communication from the leader while encouraging clear communication in return is an obvious but rare skill among leaders.

LEADERS DRAW THE BEST FROM OTHERS

If there's one thread in the leadership style conversation, it's that helping others be better at their jobs is the primary concern of all our leaders. Giving their teams the mental and emotional tools to deal with tough situations and hard challenges is part of that territory. There's no room for walking on eggshells in these situations. Leaders are expected to have a clear message for the team. What might not be that obvious is that helping others find their voice is as important as having a voice. "There's an element of radical honesty, and I don't mean that in the context of giving people feedback," says Libby Delana of Mechanica. "What I mean by that is to look at what are considered norms and putting those things through the filter of honesty. We ask, 'Do you have to continue to hold this as the way we should always do things?' So I guess it's less about, 'Here's what we know to be true,' and rather being radically honest and asking, 'But do we have to believe that it's true? And can we challenge those?'" When Delana reflects on how the people in her organization might describe her leadership style, she says, "I think probably the language they would use would be optimistic and empathetic." She pauses for a long time, and unwittingly reinforces her thoughtfulness. "I think. It's an interesting question."

The ability to find the best in others means pushing them out of their familiar thinking. To move others to a new way of thinking is a cornerstone of making them more successful. Pulling them out of their comfort zones is the job of the design leader. "It's collaborative," says John Torres, Digital Design Director at America's Test Kitchen. "Not all ideas come from a single source. I'm good at collecting ideas, listening to all sources, and seeing what works." Torres, who oversees a vast array of digital design properties and assets at the country's most respected test kitchen, realizes that collaboration isn't about telling others what to do. "It has to be done in an understanding and respectful way. Respect for the team's ideas. I try not to dismiss any ideas and remind myself that I'm not too good for anything."

When asked about her management style, Sarah Tesla from Make in Vancouver says, "Easygoing," which, when contrasted with her intense eye contact and cross-country motorbike stories, hardly seems possible. Tesla, who leads a digital design studio of 13 designers and developers, observes, "I am not a micromanager at all. I really give people the space that they need to figure out what they're doing and how they're doing it. And, yeah, I sort of feel like everyone on my team is a bit of a counselor to me, in that sense." Tesla allows the team to deliver on the details while she takes ownership of the big picture. "I keep the 10,000-feet view to give me perspective for myself. It helps me know when to step in and provide support if something's going off the rails a bit, or if I just generally see someone who still needs a little bit of work to try and get to maybe a point of confidence that they're lacking, or a skill that they're still developing. If I have something to offer there, then I'll step in and support however I can." Tesla is sensitive not to swoop in too often and come off as a micromanager. She tells the story of her creative director, whose previous roles were micromanaged. "He'd come in, he'd sit down, present an idea, and then it would be picked apart by his old boss. He always felt like he had that backseat driver. Over-the-shoulder type of management. He's mentioned to me that it's refreshing to be in an environment where that doesn't happen. Where it feels more like a mutually respectful conversation about the outcome we're trying to reach. If you have something valuable to offer, great, but you're not going to just shit on my idea before we've had a chance to figure it out." Tesla concludes with an insight that is true of all design businesses. "If you start a business and you're one person, you kind of build around you the things that relate to your personality." Personal styles influence leadership styles in so many ways. Successful leaders know which of their personal styles to nurture and which need to be changed.

One might argue that the best way to lead others to their success is to be the role model for that success. "Lead by example," says Warren Wilansky, founder of Plank in Montreal. "That's first and foremost the way I see it. In other words, I want my team to know that I am willing to do anything that they are doing. I am not above anything. I'm not above any task. I want them to feel that I'm with them and I'm just as willing to do it. And I think by doing that, people understand that leadership for me means not being separate from the team." Wilansky goes on to explain that Plank has always been a really flat organization and that his CEO role might be considered a leader by default. "I happened to be there first. I have to be the one that's the leader, but it doesn't mean that I'm above or beyond doing wherever anybody else is doing on our team."

FINAL WORDS

Leadership styles might be complex and varied, but underneath it all they all strive for the same outcome: getting the best out of the people they lead. Guiding people to being their best selves is the role of the design leader. How they get there is almost always a deeply personal journey. "Sometimes it's different for us girls," says Clockwork CEO Nancy Lyons. "We've had to embrace the word 'bossy' in the most positive of ways. The truth is uncomfortable, but I love telling the truth. I've never really thought about myself in terms of leadership but because I tell the truth, there's leadership in that. I was working in a company that recognized me as the person that most wanted to follow. I wanted to contribute to a place that I wanted to work. I'd had too many experiences working in places that weren't thoughtful. Ultimately, that means being empowering." Lyons nails the overall lesson here. Your leadership style will be a complex collection of personal characteristics and experiences. There isn't going to be an ideal leadership style because each business is different. "I really believe in the team, and my job is to be empowering and inspirational. I think my team would align with the empowering and inspirational sentiment." Apparently Lyons's advice isn't just lip service; she's walking the walk, too. "I recently got a Post-It note on my desk that said, 'You inspire me to be a better person.'"

KEY TAKEAWAYS

- Create an environment where failures can lead to personal and professional growth.

- Being a teacher-style leader to your team can be a good way to become a student.

- Lead by example. Get your hands dirty, but don't forget to also delegate.

- Nobody wants a micromanager. Find ways to return authority and create trust.

- One-on-one meetings are something you shouldn't delegate. The feedback is too valuable.

- Regardless of your style, ultimately it needs to motivate and empower your team.

- Being a good communicator also means encouraging good communication.

- Leadership means being considered as a part of the team and still being able to maintain your status as the leader.

Sales and Marketing

Introduction

Call this topic what you will—sales, business development, or new business—it all has the same outcome for design leaders: it brings home the bacon. Without a pipeline of project opportunities, the design groups we interviewed would not exist. Sales is the backbone of a for-profit organization, but healthy sales impact more than just the bottom line. A strong sales pipeline and clear marketing message boost the company's morale and motivation. In our interviews, we saw that design leaders who showed confidence in business development strategies also earned the respect of their teams and clients.

It's probably not surprising that for many, this area of the design leader's responsibility was the most problematic. For many of the leaders interviewed for this book, sales and marketing results in a lot of sleepless nights. At conferences for design leaders, like Owner Camp and Mind the Product, this topic got a lot of people's attention. It's clear that having a sales and marketing strategy that produces consistent results is a high priority. The universal concern is that the skills for building new business relationships aren't always the design leader's strongest traits. Many design leaders come from a design, engineering, or marketing background. Almost none of the leaders we interviewed had any formal training in sales. In fact, 40% admit to not being involved with sales in any direct way. This is in spite of the fact that they consider sales to be one of the most important elements of business success. It follows that the remaining 60% of design leaders believed it is senior leadership's job to do business development.

We could dedicate an entire book to this topic. There is more to cover on marketing and sales than can be adequately supported in this format. However, we decided to include this topic because it came up in almost all our interviews as a core competency of successful design leaders. Given the critical nature of developing new business opportunities, we feel that a design leader needs to develop these skills in order to bring true value to their organization. The strategies and tactics we describe are not universal elixirs for business development problems but actual methods successful design leaders have used to turn prospects into clients.

Sales and marketing are inextricably linked to one another. These days, consumers don't differentiate between the service or product and the marketing of that service or product. This is also true of buyers of design services. What the buyer reads in a blog post, which is essentially a marketing piece, is also considered to be a window into the design firm's approach to problem-solving. These insights are often referenced in sales conversations. Thought-leadership pieces, whether written, broadcasted, or delivered in person, are understood by the buyer to be stories representing the firm's approach to work. In the successful design firms that we interviewed, the salesperson role is almost always represented by a founder, CEO, lead designer/developer, or senior strategist. This person represents the company's vision, values, and process—and negotiates scope and deal dynamics. Where the marketing starts and ends is impossible to say. In our opinion, this gray area will only continue to get more ambiguous. Sales and marketing will feel like the same thing, and this is good for design leaders. Ultimately, a design leader is someone who can do the job of a marketer *and* a salesperson. She is someone who can talk about strategic solutions, build relationships with clients, and make the seamless transition to project teams. Building those relationships happens in the superficial landscape of social media as much as it does in face-to-face boardroom negotiations. Knowing this and directing efforts along a continuum of sales and marketing will bear more fruit.

Opening Up

All relationships start with the first contact. In the digital design space, those initial contacts are very often just that—digital. A blog post, a YouTube video, or an online case study might be the way a new prospect makes initial contact with design firms. It has become the norm for designers to share their ideas and thoughts with the world via articles, blogs, podcasts, and other vectors. Writing, speaking, and teaching are ultimately thought-leadership approaches. There are certainly other ways to establish your domain expertise in an area, but these activities are the most common and very often the most effective. Tracking the writing and speaking efforts to new business can sometimes be hard to do. We wondered how helpful these thought-leadership activities were and how they impacted the sales and marketing funnels for our design leader's organizations. It was clear from our interviews that sharing ideas does ultimately result in a project or something worth collaborating on with a client.

"Think of it like friendships. When you tend to share something [with some-one], that person opens themselves up," says Bryan Zmijewski, CEO of Zurb and frequent author of long-form blog posts that describe the inner workings of projects and operations at his Silicon Valley-based design firm. "You make your-self more vulnerable. People like that. They want to see more of that. So when I look at what we do as a company, we are basically making ourselves vulnerable and saying, 'Hey, this is our thinking on this.' Zmijewski believes that because this is difficult to do, most companies aren't willing to open up like this to create new relationships. Writing about the big and small issues that face his firm gives him a platform to share insights and make connections to an audience of like-minded entrepreneurs and design thinkers. His approach to connecting to new opportunities starts with understanding that everyone at Zurb is a marketer. "You're marketing through your work. You're sharing your ideas—and when you do that, people come to you. They gravitate toward you because they want to be part of that." Instead of having a traditional marketing plan, Zurb is just inten-tionally sharing their ideas and insights with the general target audience all the time. This isn't unique to Zurb. We witnessed this type of sharing in several of the top design firms we interviewed. "If you look at everything you do as market-ing, you're not specifically addressing things through techniques or tactics. It's getting good at the work, opening yourself up, creating conversations, and then creating a cycle of feedback that informs the work in a better way and allows [you] to then go back out to people and say, 'Hey, what do you think?' That cycle is what generates the marketing activity."

Sharing isn't something that happens by accident. It has to be part of the cul-ture, and the design leader needs to set the example for the rest of the team. Writing, speaking, or teaching are the most common ways for design leaders to get into the limelight. For most leaders, public writing and speaking comes with the role. Sitting in the shadows isn't an option for the leaders or the people who work for them.

Getting people to share in this way requires active effort on behalf of the leaders. Zmijewski feels that in order to be sharing something of value, it's nec-essary to have an open relationship with your team. "I constantly go to people's desks and ask, what are you doing? What are you working on? Do people need to know about that? Have you learned anything new?" says Zmijewski. "Once you start doing that regularly, you start to see patterns and you can tell people they need to share that. That's important." By building a culture around sharing, it becomes the overall expectation of the entire group. It simply becomes something you just do, and not because someone is saying you have to do it.

YOUR WORK IS YOUR MARKETING

Opening up to the world about what's going on in your organization isn't limited to domain expertise either. For some design leaders, sharing how they work, what their process is, and what they expect from their client relationships takes transparency to a whole new level. "I'm painfully transparent with our clients [about] how our sales process works," says Ben Jordan, the new coowner and CEO of nGen Works. "I had a client who came to us with a red alert project and asked who was going to be on the team. I was very honest with him and said, 'Actually, you know, we are going to hire for this. We need to hire for this specific position, but we're stepping along this path together and when you come on board, we'll then have the capital commitment from you to hire the people who we've been waiting to bring in.'" Jordan says that his clients actually really like that approach. They like the honesty about the fact that nGen is still growing and that growth will be an advantage for the client and the project. "I think the fact that we've decided to be fully open about everything has really helped." According to Jordan, the clients use this transparency to understand what he and his team are trying to do, and when they see that this thinking aligns with their own thinking, it seems to create a better relationship.

Jordan also believes that the games that are so typical of the traditional sales pitch just don't work anymore. These Mad-Men-esque pitches are typically characterized by a pitch-man telling the client why his company is better for the job than everyone else. The pitch centers on the design studio's competencies and sometimes even includes some potential solutions for the upcoming work. This approach bothers Jordan. He feels that design leaders need to truly understand why they want to work with clients. The motivations for working with clients will be transparent to the client, even when you don't say them out loud. "We don't tend to participate in RFPs,[1] simply because that process doesn't really mesh with our model." Jordan worries that pitching a client on the solution before they get to know each other is a recipe for failure. "To us, it's about the reaching out to the community. It's much more organic and casual than a concerted campaign."

---

1 RFP: Request for Proposal

For someone like Jordan who has been doing this for so long, it seems natural to him, so a formal plan might not be necessary. If you're just starting out, then developing a plan that reinforces these outreach routines might be required.

Attracting interesting clients through developing highly focused relationships was a common theme in the interviews. Some of these relationships are based on industry, and some on affinity. "To be honest, we have never done a great job of marketing our services using the normal outbound marketing avenues," admits Dave Valliere, CEO of Velir. "But what we have done a really good job about since the early days is partnering with our existing clients." Valliere, whose team of designers and developers numbered 120 at the time of our meeting, explains what that client conversation looks like. "We're talking to our clients and [taking] the long view. This is really important to us. That means both the investment that we make in the organization but also the approach that we bring to our partner engagements with clients. When we're talking about onboarding a new account, we're already thinking about what the next three years look like with this organization. We ask them questions around what they are interested in doing beyond just this one project." Opening the conversation to discuss values and long-term ambitions connects the design organization with the client's team in a way that a credentials pitch can't compare with. In today's transparent business environment, clients want to know who they are dealing with. They are not just interested in the superficial details like team size and awards won. They want to understand the overall vision of the company and the core values of their new design partners.

This long-term view isn't shared by all design leaders, but it's a view we endorse and recommend. For project-based design groups, this isn't always going to fit into their sales lens. But for almost all design organizations, it encourages the team to get focused on the relationship and not just the immediate work in front of them.

Valliere goes on to describe how these relationships pay off over the long term. "We feel like that first project is the opportunity for our clients to really get to know us as an organization and [see] what we value and how we can work with them, but it sets the stage for a longer relationship. As a result, we've been able to partner with clients for many years. Some clients we've been working with, really, since May of 2000, and we continue to do work with them. We have done several rebranding and redesigns of their websites over the years." The benefits of these ongoing relationships will also transcend trends and technologies. "It's transcended many different leadership changes at their organization. And they've always found the value of working with Velir through the last 15 years."

This last point is critical to both the client-relationship success and to the organizational success. Valliere reinforces what we stated earlier: that marketing and sales are not separate. Creating business development strategies that are connected to the core of who you are and what you do is critical to building successful long-term relationships. Having a vision and values that transcend time allow you to connect to your clients in spite of changes at their organizations or in the market. This connection between the design organization's core culture and the relationship the client is looking for allows successful leaders to persist over time without getting tripped up on issues linked to a specific trend, technology, or client leadership change. If you are connected to the outcomes, and not the superficial technologies, your marketing and sales lens will stand the test of time.

"When you're thinking about that partnership with the client beyond just the project that's in front of you, you start making decisions that are more around the long view," explains Valliere. "What is it going to look like beyond this project? And you start making decisions that are more based around what's in their best interests, rather than when you're just looking at what the next quarter looks like or what this individual project means from a profit perspective." A smart design leader might choose to take small concessions on that first project, knowing that that's setting the stage for more work down the line. These concessions show the client you're interested in developing that relationship and not just focused on closing the deal. At this early stage, the design leader is signaling to the client that they are are not only a good agency to work with now but also in the future. At Fresh Tilled Soil, we have discovered through a decade of selling design that most of the real opportunities are beyond that initial project. To ensure longevity for a team, getting into those upcoming opportunities is the ultimate goal.

Aligning Marketing with Mission

Authentic and transparent marketing messages aren't just fashionable; they are essential to success. As we heard from nGen's Ben Jordan earlier, whether we choose to be transparent or not matters, and it seems to matter more than ever. What might not be immediately obvious is that in a social-media-driven and highly connected marketplace, our partners, team members, and clients will see through all the opaque sales tricks and see us for what we really are anyway.

There's nowhere to hide. Being open and transparent isn't just an advantage—it's becoming a requirement of good relationship development.

Being transparent starts with understanding what you want from your relationships with your partners and clients. Knowing your reasons for being helps you craft the right type of conversation to have with your clients.

"I feel like we're very clear about our sense of purpose right now," says Steven Fitzgerald of the Habanero Consulting Group in Vancouver. "We articulate our purpose in this pithy little way. *We're very passionate about helping people in our organizations thrive.* I know that sounds very generic, but it's super meaningful to us and it's getting more and more meaningful over time." When your purpose or mission is clear to the team, it's very likely going to be clear for the client as well. Fitzgerald believes that actively sharing your mission or purpose with the larger community, which includes your clients, reduces the friction that sometimes characterizes new business relationships. Alignment between the design studio's values and the client's values is what smooths out the friction.

Alignment has its challenges, too. Finding alignment and keeping it are two different things. Fitzgerald warns that the worst mistake a design leader can make is allowing the company's purpose to be pulled off track by a client's desire to do things that are not core to the business. Once the leadership has identified a sweet spot in which to operate and articulated a clear vision for getting there, it's essential that they don't stray. Fitzgerald encourages leaders to defend their focus on their sweet spot. It keeps the internal organization aligned but it has the added benefit of keeping your marketing message clear and understood. The biggest threat to this focus is from the very people they are targeting with the marketing and sales messages. "Your clients, being well meaning and even supportive, will say 'You guys are so good at this thing; can you help us with this other thing?' Being drawn away from the stuff that we're great at and passionate about has been the continual challenge for us." Knowing what you're good at and knowing what to turn away from is not just an operational choice; it's your brand position. Frequently, design leaders are lured to opportunities that don't fall into their area of focus. The promise of a new business doing something not quite in their wheelhouse is a constant siren. At Fresh Tilled Soil, we refer to this as "the competency trap." Just because you're good at doing something doesn't mean you should be doing it. Your choice of values and purpose is not just how you create culture and align operations; it's your marketing story.

Determining a clear path and aligning your messages and energy behind that path are more than just philosophies. They are simply good for business. "When I look at the financial profit, growth, and engagement, and the sort of quantifiable elements of business success, or compare it to how my gut feels, it's actually quite clear when we are in that sweet spot of what we care about, what we're passionate about, and what we're good at," says a very passionate Steven Fitzgerald. "When we're living our purpose, we're killing it in the market. We're growing at the rate we want to grow at. We're highly profitable. People are happy. Clients are super happy. It's freaking nirvana." Fitzgerald's enthusiasm isn't unique either. This alignment between purpose and business outcomes is something that's noticeable in all the successful design firms we met with. When these companies are aligning with their core values, they have stronger sales pipelines, lower staff turnover, higher revenues, and wider margins.

There's some debate as to how this alignment develops. For our design leaders, providing the vision for their marketing direction was sometimes deliberate and sometimes happenstance. Not all of the leaders had hard and fast marketing plans. Detailed plans might not be everyone's approach, but what was common to successful leaders was they all had a very clear vision. What's more, they knew how to translate that vision into action. "New business is an ongoing challenge," says Libby Delana of Mechanica. "For us, it's a little bit more organic than systematized. We do have a plan and a strategy. We also have a goal of the kinds of business we'd really love to work on. Half that list are organizations that really inspire us and that inherently tickle a passion point." Aligning with their client's vision provides a compatibility where the people that work together have more in common than just the work. Their values and interests are aligned. This has one more advantage that Delana notes: "I do think there's something interesting in this alignment because in our 10 years in business … a lot of clients, as they moved from one company to another, [have] brought us with them." Delana believes that once alignment has been established with a client, it doesn't fade. Although Delana feels that the best sales strategy is understanding the inherent overlaps of interest between her organization and the client organization, she still takes the time to create a strategy to get there. Leaving marketing to chance is just too risky for service organizations.

Alignment is just another form of focus. Marketing to and working with clients who are not in your wheelhouse might seem like a good idea initially, but it's a slippery slope. "There are times when we're outside of that sweet spot," says Habanero's Fitzgerald. "We're doing stuff that seemed like a good idea and seemed like a good opportunity, but it's not what we care about. It's not where we're going to make an impact on our clients. It's not where we're going to change their organizations in a meaningful way." Working outside of their area of focus not only reduces Habanero's ability to impact their clients but also reduces their ability to change their own organization in positive ways. "Our learning goes down. Our ability to innovate recedes." Put simply, a lack of clarity about vision or purpose reduces what you care about and results in poor marketing, misaligned client projects, and internal disorder.

For design firms, there is an easy balance between taking on new work to keep the cash flow healthy and selecting the best possible work for the team's morale. The ability to find this balance isn't easy when you're starting out, but it seems to improve with time. "It's often discussed that we pick the best clients or are very selective of the clients we work with, which is true to an extent," says Brian Williams of Viget, whose company numbers around 70 people across three offices. "But, at the end of the day, we are a big company and we have a lot of mouths to feed. It's a lot of expenses to figure out. We never forget that the fact that somebody's coming into our organization [and] is willing to write a big check for us to do the things that we love to do is just a truly great thing to have happen. So we are very, very appreciative of that and try not to take too arrogant a stance of 'this isn't exactly the right project at the right time,' that kind of thing."

A continued focus on finding the right clients and a healthy balance between financial needs and alignment with purpose pays off for many. The disclaimer is that this payoff never comes quickly. Almost all our successful design leaders have been running their businesses or design groups for several years. "We are certainly selective about clients," says Williams. "If we think a project is going to be an unhappy situation for both sides, we'll walk away. We want to make sure that there's a good chance of success. Now we are at the point where a lot of [our] clients are dream clients. If you had said 10 years ago [that] we'd be working with these types of groups, I would have thought you were crazy. It's very rewarding to work hard for 15 years and get to that point." With focus comes the need for patience. There are almost no overnight successes in the design agency world.

Organizing for Optimal Outcomes

Beyond aligning your values and vision with the right type of client is the need for a plan. Being transparent and deliberate about who you work with is not enough. Especially as the organization grows, so too does the requirement to delegate some of the sales and marketing functions to people not at the senior leadership level. Delegating these responsibilities isn't always a line function. All members of the organization will have touch points with prospects and clients. As Bryan Zmijewski alluded to earlier in this chapter, "Everyone is in marketing." This means that a clear strategy for sales and marketing needs to be communicated. A plan that can create opportunities even when the design leader isn't available. "I'm a big fan of the Predictable Revenue model,"[2] says Aurimas Adomavicius, President of the Devbridge Group, referring to the book by the same name. "The idea behind the book is that you need to establish various channels of how you're going to acquire business. There is going to be inbound business that is coming in because of the previous work you've done, like referrals. There should also be outbound, which is marketing and content generation to drive interest."

Adomavicius, along with six cofounders, runs a fast-growing 120-person design and development firm in Chicago, IL. This growth is no accident. Supporting a large team isn't something Adomavicius wants to leave to chance. His approach toward business development is one of the more structured we came across. "For all of the different inbound and outbound channels, you need to have three different tiers of individuals processing the incoming business. So you have the hunters who go out and bring in the leads. They don't necessarily close the business, but they go out there and establish those relationships and have the initial discussions. You have the closers, which are folks that are typically more mature and sophisticated in how they do things. They understand the strategy component much better. Then you also have the last piece, which is the farmers, the individuals, typically like account execs and so on, who work within the account to make sure the customer is happy and that they continue doing business, potentially even expanding the footprint within the organization." Breaking down the components of the business development funnel into layers is ideal, but not all organizations have the people to do that. Smaller firms need to have someone who can wear several hats and fill multiple roles.

In our own experience at Fresh Tilled Soil, we've noticed that sales and marketing work better when they are integrated with each other in some way. At the highest level, this is the clearly communicated vision and values of the organization from the very top. "For the strategic and company direction, I think that the leaders of the organization have to do the majority of that work," warns Adomavi-

---

2 Ross, Aaron and Marylou Tyler. *Predictable Revenue: Turn Your Business Into a Sales Machine with the $100 Million Best Practices of Salesforce.com* PebbleStorm, 2011.

cius. "I don't think you can hire an outsider to know exactly what you're trying to do with the business. It has to come from top down." The next responsibility from the design leader is to make sure the sales and marketing people are frequently talking to each other. Coordinating their communication and actions is critical to a focused approach.

THOUGHT LEADERSHIP IS YOUR MARKETING

"Marketing is that outbound piece," says Adomavicius. "I look at marketing as having two functions. One function is how we position ourselves. This covers things like: how do we talk about our company, what services are we going to offer, and what verticals are we going to target for each of our services. That's just defining the brand itself and the strategy for the brand. The second function is actually doing specific outbound campaigns. Outbound campaigns could be trade shows. They could be email campaigns. They could be blog topics that target specific service areas." Tactically, the campaigns should be directed at specific audiences that have been identified as good prospects. As we heard from the design leaders before, there's no use targeting an audience that promises financial gains alone. The marketing campaigns to your ideal audience should be backed up with examples and case studies of successful work in that vertical area. Developing content that connects you to these target clients will allow you to acquire audience attention. In other words, talk about the things that are meaningful to these clients and to your organization in order to have the biggest chance of reaching them.

Finding focus for your outreach can be hard at first. In fact, most design leaders struggle with staying focused even when their organizations are mature. Experimentation might be required but most leaders agree that developing thought leadership content in your specific domain is the key. "I would say the first year was just shooting anything in any direction I could possibly think of. I tried everything," reflects Ross Beyeler, founder of Cambridge, MA-based ecommerce strategy and design firm Growth Spark. "Whether it was networking or begging people or writing an article or paying for ads, I just literally tried everything. I just wanted to see what would stick. Over the years, I think that we found three particular areas that work really well for us. The first is our focus on content from the perspective of thought leadership as opposed to just for SEO purposes." This type of content focuses on setting up the design leadership as thought leaders. The content, when correctly executed, can be published on other authoritative blogs and resources that point back to the firm to demonstrate their experience in the space. "That's been a huge driver for us, especially in the last … year and a half, two years," says Beyeler.

"The second is a lot of teaching," continues Beyeler. "We actually do a lot of workshops with partners like Shopify, which is the platform we use. We do a lot with educational platforms like General Assembly, which is a continuing education organization. We even do some teaching with traditional colleges like Babson." Beyeler is confident that the teaching has been helpful, not so much in terms of pure lead generation, but as an opportunity where his team can meet the people that they might one day work with, either as clients or employees. "We have conversations with [them] and give them an opportunity to sit in on one of our free workshops. This way, they get to know us and get to know our style better, and learn something in the process. That's actually been a big way to help drive conversion for us in terms of potential deals.

"The last area is the community. We focus on two communities with a series of events for both," describes Beyeler. "One event is called Managing an Agency Business; the other is called Managing an E-Commerce Business. They're both built around the same model. Three or four times a year, we put on an event for these groups." Beyeler and his team recruit a panelist of experts, either agency owners or e-commerce entrepreneurs, to come in and speak about the experiences they've had and things that they've learned in their respective space. According to Beyeler, they will usually see somewhere around 50 to 75 people attending the event. "We'll use those events to foster a community for agency owners and for e-commerce entrepreneurs here in Boston. It's been a great way for us to … maintain a presence but also to have the opportunity to introduce interesting people to other interesting people."

Community-aligned events and activities are common in the design industry. For many design leaders, the choice to get involved with the community has already been made for them when they choose their domain or technology focus. "We decided to deprecate our own efforts to build a custom CMS and instead plow them into the Drupal community," says Tiffany Farriss of Palantir. "It was that decision to adopt open source, initially in an agnostic kind of way, that lead us to this decision." Initially Farriss and her copartner were on the fence about which technology to support, but once they realized the power of the Drupal community, the decision was easy. "Within a year, we we had made the commitment that we weren't going to do anything that's not open source. Getting involved in the open source community and throwing all of our experience, energy, passion, and enthusiasm behind that—that's really been the driver for our pipeline."

As mentioned by Aurimas Adomavicius, it's always a good idea to build multiple channels and not to rely too much on one channel for leads. For several years, Palantir's inbound pipeline was fueled by these community contributions, whether just the straight code contributions or contributions to camp or conferences. "We were very, very fortunate to grow with a primarily passive sales pipeline," says Farriss. "As we've grown, though, we're now at the point where we need to develop a more mature sales process and so we're starting some outbound efforts and things like that, but that's very new for us." Nothing is static in business. What works today may not work tomorrow. Developing several channels for leads is not just prudent; it's a requirement of success.

Converting Leads to Deals

Outreach efforts create a general funnel for leads, but those leads aren't business yet. In their simplest form, leads are just opportunities to have a conversation with a prospect about their project. We wondered what the best design leaders do once those leads come in. "I handle all of them," says Beyeler. "My rule is that no one's too big or too small to have at least a [short] conversation with. So [we] always schedule a call. [We] won't necessarily jump right into a meeting just for efficiency's sake, but we'll definitely have a first call just to run through what they're trying to accomplish. We're extremely focused in what we do, so it's often that we can just, in that first conversation, kind of jump to a high-level yes or no where we're not going to stall around. Either we do exactly what they need or we don't, and if we don't, I make it a habit to at least make one to three introductions to people I know and trust [that] through the MAB[3] community [someone can probably] help them. So that's a big thing I think that's helped us: being focused on helping our potential clients find a solution, whether it's with us or not, [with] as much focus as we have on actually trying to close the deal."

Beyeler's approach to hands-on sales is not unique. We witnessed top design leaders rolling up their sleeves to stay involved in sales from initial contact to client onboarding. The importance of the design leader in the front-line sales role cannot be overstated. Whether it's in the job description or not, the top executive at a design firm is also the top salesperson. "It's still a huge focus for me. And it

---

3 MAB: Managing an Agency Business (*http://mab.growthspark.com/*): A community of digital agency owners that meet several times a year to discuss issues affecting senior agency people.

always will be," says Joe Rinaldi, President of Happy Cog. "I don't see that changing substantially. I really don't. I think sales for us is a team sport. It's not one person's sole responsibility. There are a lot of moving pieces that we intentionally involve so that the entire team is really invested in and cares about sales. It's more orchestration and making sure that people are contributing and not overlapping [and that] people are heard and not shouted over." Using this inclusive approach and leading by example has been Rinaldi's key to creating a company where people at all levels happily and willfully contribute to the sales process.

From the prospect or client point of view, having the design leader involved in new business conversations is meaningful. If you're the client about to commit hundreds of thousands of dollars and your team's resources to a project, it helps to be able to sit across the table and talk about that with the design leader. "I feel like the owner of a company is the best salesperson for that company," confirms Ben Jordan. "I've seen it make a difference time after time. The sales impact scales with the passion of the owner. I'm fortunate to be president and owner of the company so it's my vision we're executing, and I think people can see that passion. People can understand when you're really actually caring about solving their problem versus meeting a sales quota."

Having the most senior people participating in sales doesn't mean they are 100% responsible for sales. The design leaders are involved in the conversations but they are supported by a team of salespeople, project managers, and domain experts to get the deals done. No person is an island but having the senior leader at the negotiating table carries significant weight. "I don't ever want to get to a point where I don't have a substantial role in this, unless there's a new president of Happy Cog and that person is the one leading the charge," says Happy Cog's Rinaldi. "If you're a client coming in to talk about a project and you're talking to someone at the middle of the organization, you feel differently than if the owner or leader is there representing the team. Personally, if I have to go up against somebody else whose name is pretty synonymous with their design shop, I would feel a lot less influential than that person if I didn't have a comparable title and a perceived comparable role in the organization. I don't think it's something that will ever go away, frankly."

CEO AS CHIEF SALES OFFICER

Successful leaders of design companies take their role in sales seriously because they know it's the lifeblood of their business. Having a great portfolio and a strong team of talented people is no longer enough. You need to be face-to-face with the client, discussing solutions to their problems. "In this phase of the company, it's me leading sales with a team under me supporting the administrative tasks like contract creation and meeting scheduling," says Jordan. "But I am the one giving the pitches. I am the one making the promises, because I want to make sure that we are connecting with the client."

"I do focus a lot on sales and marketing of our own agency," says Geoff Wilson, CEO of 352 Inc., an 85-person design agency. "I actually feel that's been one of the things that has helped us grow. Specifically, I am a very, very poor designer and I'm a very, very poor developer. In the early days, when we first started back in the late 1990s, I could do just enough HTML and just enough Photoshop work to get us by, but it was really not great quality and soon I started hiring people who were a heck of a lot better than me." It's not uncommon for design leaders to get their start as technicians. They start out designing and developing, but adapt to leadership roles out of necessity. That includes selling and marketing leadership.

Wilson makes a point that hints at the maturity required by design leaders. "It was very easy for me to remove myself from those roles and concentrate on the business side of things. I actually think that because of the fact that I have a failed design and development career, it forced me to really focus on the growth of the agency, which has been good for the agency's ability to grow." This seems more likely to be driven by Wilson's knowledge that it's more important for his business that he focus on sales and marketing than continue to be a designer or developer. However you look at it, design and development are the commodities of the design industry. The strategic power comes when a leader aligns themselves with the activities that generate new opportunities and grow the firm's reputation. "I think a lot of smaller agencies can sometimes have a founder coming from a very creative background or sometimes a very technical background and that person loves that craft. There's absolutely nothing wrong with that—that's wonderful, but typically, those agencies are going to stay more boutique in terms of size because the owner wants to continue to be involved with the craft. They want to continue to design or develop and again, [there's] nothing wrong with that. I think for an agency to grow, the owner has to remove themselves from the day-to-day craft, at least to a large extent, and focus on things like business development."

In cases where a large part of the lead filtering is going through the most senior person in the organization, scaling this task might be a concern. If design leaders are taking on responsibility for business development, then what happens when the company grows and more is expected of them? "Granted, if you are a bigger organization, one person doesn't scale as a sales team. I'm a firm believer that, as the leader of a company and the head vision guy, I need to be a part of every sales cycle so that our clients see my passion for what we are building."

Being involved doesn't mean doing it all. The answer to scaling is not to try to do it all but to understand what the process looks like and to make it more efficient. "When it comes to scaling anything, I usually try to figure out where the opportunity is to create more of a process as opposed to throwing more bodies at the problem," says Beyeler. "So instead of saying, 'Oh well, I just need more sales people,' it's usually of question of 'Okay, how can I make my sales process better so that I'm more effective at doing it?' because it's going to be pretty hard for me to find someone else who is familiar with this industry, who understands what we do, who knows how *we* do it, and [who] can sell in a way that we do." By figuring out how to scale performance as opposed to scaling the number of bodies associated with delivering sales, firms like Beyeler's have continued to grow without needing a large sales team.

Scaling performance means really looking at the types of conversations your business needs to have to close deals. This requires knowing what the common questions are during those conversations so you're prepared with the right answers. Finding a way to frontload the initial conversations with the right expectations will save time. Projects that are not a good fit will be immediately identified, so you can decide whether to invest more time or walk away. Cutting through the noise as quickly as possible so you can focus on helping them find the right partner, whether it's your firm or not. "If we know there are certain things that are just bottlenecks later on in the sales process, whether it's timing or budget or technology, we try to just bring that up right away," says Beyeler. "So that way two or three weeks later, when we're finally sitting down and getting into the details, we're not shocked by anything."

IMPROVING SALES BY TURNING AWAY BUSINESS

Part of the filtering process also means turning away work and/or helping prospects find better-suited partners. We heard time and time again from design leaders about how they would help prospects that they were sure would never be a good match. They passed on the leads to other agencies or provided insights that would help these prospects make better choices about their project.

"We've honestly had situations where people have come back months later, or even years later, [and] they say, 'Hey. Thank you for introducing me to that person. They were great. I'm doing a new thing. I'd love to talk to you again.'"

Compassion for their prospects and a genuine interest in making them successful is good karma. You don't have to be a social scientist to know that if you're helping people out, they will remember you with fondness. "There's been a lot of that kind of karma payback—simply by focusing on helping people find who's going to be the best for their project, even if that's not necessarily us."

This compassion extends to existing projects as well. Your best future client is also the client you're working with right now. As my father, who was a salesperson, would say, "It's way easier to top up the bucket than to have to fill it up from scratch each month." Investing in your current client allows you to invest in your pipeline. "Do a great job with your customers so they come back, so they're loyal," says Dave Gray of XPLANE. "And also ask them to help you build relationships within the organization. The majority of our growth comes from somebody that we've done something successful for.... The word gets around or we're referred [to someone else]." Gray feels that the things that keep his business on a relatively steady growth path are doing a great job for customers and getting continuous feedback. He isn't afraid to ask for the business. "By just being straightforward and asking people, 'If you are happy with the job that we did, we would be very grateful for you to introduce us to people in the organization.'"

Gray adds a cautionary note. "You don't want to have the kind of company that's dependent on one client. If they go away you're going to lose half your business. So another policy that we have is to never have more than 20 percent of our business from any one customer." His experience has taught him that this is an easy trap to fall into. We saw this error in several cases during our interviews where studios were heavily invested in one or two client projects. This dependence can happen to companies that are not geared up to develop a consistent sales pipeline. It's easy to get overly focused on the work you have and forget about what happens when a project comes to an end. Investing in a long-term sales pipeline even while turning away mismatched business might seem counterintuitive, but it's the strategy most often associated with successful sales cycles.

Salespeople, Commissions, and Incentives

Although 60% of the design leaders we interviewed were heavily involved in the new-business cycle at their firms, several also relied on dedicated salespeople. These salespeople took many different forms, from traditional business development pavement-pounders to strategists that met with prospects to shepherd them through the buying process. These roles also differed in terms of seniority but very few successful design leaders left salespeople to operate without their support. At Fresh Tilled Soil, we committed to having a senior full-time salesperson as soon as we could. Our current head of sales was the fourth employee to join the company. This might seem surprising for what was then a small design agency, but our logic was, and remains today, that without a senior-level dedicated salesperson we wouldn't have the consistency of sales to build a strong foundation for cash flow. Cash is the lifeblood of any business. For service companies like design studios that can't rely on outside funding, its importance cannot be overstated.

There is a lot of great literature on motivating salespeople so we don't feel it necessary to repeat what's been said elsewhere. Our design leaders have broadly differing views on how to incentivize their salespeople. There really isn't a generic approach to providing the right carrots for individuals or teams to make them push harder. What was common among the experienced design leaders was their lack of affection for commission-based incentives. "As a service business, we aren't able to scale quickly around new business. We have to stack it up into the future," says Jed Banner from SmallBox. "This can be frustrating for a commissioned salesperson—having to sell next quarter and not get commission until invoicing." Along with hiring cycles being connected to new projects, linking rewards to far-off timelines can frustrate salespeople and their leaders.

For the organization, commissions are equally problematic. If a salesperson is motivated entirely by a commission, their goals will not be aligned with the company's goals. If the company's objective is to bring in a certain type of project but the salesperson feels that other types will increase their potential commission, you have a misaligned sales strategy. Seen from the other side, it's not possible for the salesperson to be successful if they don't see rewards for the projects they are told to pursue. "We don't want our sales team to be motivated to drag in whatever business they can find," continues Banner. "To do great work, we need great clients. And we have become increasingly picky about client and scope, with good results all around. A commissioned sales team is often focused on the money and not the fit. I need them wired for fit." As we discussed earlier in this chapter, alignment between company and client is essential. What's less obvious is having the studio team aligned for a common purpose. In the decades we've been in this industry, we've witnessed design leaders saying one thing to their salespeople but providing incentives that encourage a different outcome. Just because commissions work for some companies doesn't mean they work for design organizations. Hiring and incentivizing salespeople needs to be done at the level of the company purpose, not bottom-line outcomes.

By far, the best salespeople are those who are the most invested in the business. This often means the owners, founders, or leadership of the organization, but there are exceptions. A great salesperson is generally motivated by something more than money. They are often excited about moving people from one mindset to another. Rewards and recognition can't be ignored, but a true salesperson is someone who likes the thrill of the deal and the excitement of working with a prospect. In a way, they are similar to other domain experts in that they want to master their craft. This desire to be a master craftsperson of the sales trade is what drives the authentic salesperson. Make no mistake, money and recognition play into this success, but only as the cherry on top. Contributing to the team's success and being treated as an important part of the relationship with the client is what drives the ideal salesperson. As Banner observes, "Seeing others benefit from their efforts may be as meaningful as individual compensation."

Sales and Marketing Pipelines

If our interviews are anything to go by, leaders spend a lot of time thinking about where the next project will come from. Although there is no single way to do business development or marketing, our leaders all develop several channels to keep their pipelines full of opportunities. Having multiple channels is necessary to develop a healthy pipeline. For some early stage leaders, it can be a surprise to learn that many of the traditional sales channel approaches no longer work or have limited impact on the bottom line. What's less surprising is that successful design leaders are always connecting the dots between sales and marketing activities.

"We have a few members of our sales team who have initial conversations with the clients and work on presentations and that type of thing," says 352 Inc.'s Geoff Wilson. "But [for] any significant opportunity, they either bring me ... or one of the other senior members of our leadership team [in on the deal]. We spend a lot of time trying to cultivate opportunities when they come about." Making the connection to the bigger marketing sales picture is an important part of this life cycle. Wilson doesn't believe in relying on referrals alone. "Historically, most of our leads have come through [the] way of inbound marketing. You always hear agencies say word of mouth and referral and we've had a fair share of word of mouth and referrals over time, but we've actually also seen quite a bit of success over the years with our own search engine presence in terms of organic search engine rankings and also in terms of paid search. Paid search can be tough in terms of ROI but it has proven to be successful for us, and organic search has typically been good for us. It can produce a number of lower-quality opportunities, so you have to be willing to do a good job of prequalifying during the sales process and screening out lower-quality opportunities. But if you're willing to do that screening work, then you can find some real gems. Some of our largest accounts have actually come to us by way of finding us organically by the search engines." The filtering process is also never random at successful design firms. Once the lead comes in, it must go through an assessment to determine if it's worth pursuing or not.

"Traditional sales thinking puts all the emphasis on stuffing the top of the sales funnel with as many prospects as possible," says Robert Glazer, CEO of Acceleration Partners, a digital marketing firm in Boston. "Without malice, marketers often suggest that if you cast your net wide and slowly percolate your prospects, you'll ultimately distill fully fledged customers. This is just not the case." While having more prospects appears to be a good thing, it distracts from the importance of focusing the limited time and resources that most design leaders have. The most successful design leaders interviewed for this book relied on more focused approaches to sales. Finding the balance between highly focused activities and developing multiple channels can seem confusing and even counterintuitive at first glance. A more detailed explanation of these approaches is something we pushed for in our conversations. "There is a solution," continues Glazer, who coauthored the initial article that we wrote on this subject several years ago. "The catch is that it requires patience and flexibility. This is not a quick fix. It's based on the understanding that saying 'no' to the wrong clients can do as much for your business as getting the right clients."

Although the leaders we met with used different explanations, many of them referred to this process as a focusing tool. We call this strategy "the lens" and, when executed correctly, it is a powerful strategy for driving and sustaining profitable business. The lens, as the name implies, is a way to focus all your sales and marketing efforts. The most successful organizations are not those chasing multiple customer audiences. They focus on only one audience: the one that delivers the most profit with the least aggravation. They whittle down the distractions so that the definition of the customer can be drawn through the eye of a needle.

Creating Your Own Sales Lens

In some cases, this process can be described from the point of view of the company, but we observed that design leaders prefer to approach this problem by putting the client at the center of the conversation. This is probably because they are already in a client-centric mode, but it's also easier to get to the core of the issue, which is "Who do you want to work with and where can you deliver value?" Building a lens for your business starts with analyzing who your ideal clients already are. If you are a new company and don't have any existing clients, then create a profile of the ideal client and be prepared to modify it once you have real data. As an example, ask yourself:

- Is our ideal customer new to the market or an established business? Which do you prefer?

- Who will be making the decisions? Do you want to deal directly with the founder or CEO? Or would you rather work with big brands and deal with line managers and mid-level decision makers?

- How much experience does this client have in your field? Are you more comfortable with novices or a client who's an old hat at the game?

- What communication style do you prefer? Are you a quiet introvert who likes mild-mannered clients, or do you prefer fast-talking extroverts? Is email or phone better for you?

Go back and look at your best engagements and figure out what the successful projects/clients had in common. Also analyze what happened with the projects that did not work out well. Use this data to further focus your sales lens. Also, make sure you are aware of what economic drivers keep you profitable. You should communicate your payment terms clearly and seek clients who respect and agree to these terms without haggling.

PUTTING THE SALES LENS TO USE

Here is a high-level example of the lens that we have used to determine whether to take on a client or project. It is divided into three parts: client qualities, sales process, and other considerations.

Desirable client/project qualities

1. Client has worked with another service firm successfully and/or values an expert design partner relationship.

2. Client knows what they don't know. In other words, they respect the designer's knowledge and experience.

3. Client agrees with proven design methodologies and processes.

4. If the client has strong opinions on approaches, they get those on the table early in the relationship.

5. Client's communication style is the same or similar to the design firm's.

6. Our deliverables are not tied to people that we can't control.

In addition, if a major operational effort is going to be required from our company, the project needs to have a high mandate from client management, and the implementation team needs to understand what we are doing and be able to keep up.

Ideal sales process

1. Client values our time and demonstrates this in the proposal process.

2. The sale proceeds fairly and quickly (endless back and forth is a big red flag).

3. Client signs contract on time and makes timely deposit (we have found this to be a high predictor of future payment issues).

4. The project meets our financial criteria.

Other considerations

1. A repeat client is worth much more than a new one.

2. A referral from a trusted person or past client usually makes for a better client.

Your sales lens will have to be adjusted over time to remain effective. After encountering new information or recovering from a disastrous client relationship, figure out what went wrong and adjust the lens. On the other end of the spectrum, reflect on projects that worked out flawlessly and add those qualities as well. Keep in mind that the outliers—the best and worst potential clients—are usually easy to identify. What will really make a difference is if you can learn to discern the pros and cons of companies that are on the fringe of the middle. Although your gut will often tell you that something is not going to work out, unless you get comfortable with the borders of your lens, the inclination is often to move forward. Our biggest regrets have come from engagements where we overlooked or ignored the warning signs, or decided that we could live with one or two qualities that were outside our lens because we didn't want to turn down work. Most of those engagements were regrettable and unprofitable.

Saying no to prospective clients and projects outside your lens is what will make your business more successful. In the pharmaceutical business, the most profitable companies aren't those with the publicized blockbusters—they are the ones with the best yield, spending the fewest resources on the prospects that never make it to market. Said more simply, they are quick to kill what's likely to be a loser. Difficult clients and bad projects offset more profitable jobs and waste energy. Using the lens will ensure you spend more time doing what you do best.

THE LENS IN ACTION

Apart from our own design firm, Fresh Tilled Soil, there are several other industry leaders that rely on a filtered and focused approach to sales and marketing. Reducing market reach and selecting specific target markets has the paradoxical effect of producing better results. Knowing who to go after is half the battle. "In terms of the specific campaigns, that's more tactical," says Aurimas Adomavicius. "For example, we identify financial services as a vertical for us because we're making good progress there. We have examples that we can talk about, case studies." Adomavicius recommends a marketing approach to generate specific vertically focused content that is attractive to the target audience. This content drives engagement and leads to conversations that result in more work. This focus on a single market creates a virtuous circle where these projects generate additional similar projects, and reinforce the company's reputation in that space.

Below is a model of how these filters work based on the feedback we received in our questionnaires and interviews. We observed several similar approaches, but this structure represents the best objective approach to sales filtering. In this example, the answers are weighted to ensure they provide the right level of information. Not all information is treated equally. For example, knowing why a lead came in is just as important as knowing where the lead came from. In the model described below, the higher the score, the better the potential outcome.

Lead Origins:

1. Where did this lead or opportunity come from? Marketing effort +2; Personal or professional network +1; Web form 0; Phone call +1; Conference or event +1; Web search 0

2. If the lead was a result of a marketing effort, was the prospect able to remember what they were responding to? Yes +1; No 0

Domain and Understanding:

1. Is this potential client in an industry we understand or could quickly understand? Yes +1; No -1

2. Does this potential client have any experience designing or building web products? Yes +2; No -2

3. Does this potential client have any experience working with a design firm like ours? Yes +1; No -1

4. If the answer to #3 is yes, was that experience like for them? Very Good +2; Neutral 0; +1; Bad -1; Very Bad -2

5. If this prospect is a startup, does the team have any significant experience running a business? Yes +1; No -2

Budgeting:

1. Does this prospect have a budget or allocated funds for this project? Yes +1; No -2

2. If this is a startup, do they already have their funding secured? Yes +2; No -2

3. If this is a startup, did they offer equity in exchange for the work? Yes -2; No 0

4. Is the prospect willing to share the details of the budget with you? Yes +1; No -1

5. If the answer to #4 is no, is this because they feel you'll spend it all if you know what it is? Yes -2; No 0

6. Are they willing to enter into a Deep Dive or Strategy phase to determine the scope? Yes +2; No -2

Client Team and Resources:

1. Does the prospect have a clear vision of the business objectives? Yes +1; No -1

2. Does the prospective company have dedicated resources that will manage this project from their side? Yes +1; No -1

3. Do the individuals managing the project have relevant experience working with designers or product design firms? Yes +1; No -1

Challenge and Creativity:

1. Is this a challenging and fun project that we'd be excited to work on? Yes +2; No -2

2. Will it be hard to sell this project internally? Yes -1; No +1

3. Will we get added value from working on this project? Yes +2; No -2

You'll notice that not all questions are equally weighted. For example, we've noticed that companies with no experience working with designers or design firms are the most likely to be problematic. Lack of understanding about process, confusion about value, and a perception that a design firm is just a vendor and not a partner are some of the problems we observed when working with first-time buyers of design services.

In our experience, and from what we've observed in sophisticated design companies, sales and marketing are inextricably linked but the specific roles should be divided. For companies that are looking for consistent opportunities and would like long-term visibility into their sales pipeline, a full-time marketing person (or team) is worth their weight in gold. In larger design studios, it's advisable to have a marketing team made up of two or more full-time people. One person focuses on the website content, event planning, and gifts and the other person focuses on working with the designers and developers to create content for publications, building relationships with conference organizers, and finding speakers for events.

Every company is unique, so how they structure the sales team will depend on the size of the projects and the sales cycles. For larger or mature design firms, the goal is to get the bigger projects that offer their teams the highest rewards. For smaller businesses, it might be sufficient for the founder or owner to manage the entire sales cycle. Most small design businesses see their leads generated by referrals. This means their primary salesperson is fielding inbound calls but not making any outbound calls. Even those firms with a dedicated new business team may not need to be doing active sales in the traditional sense. Their chief activity is to follow up on inbound leads, discuss future projects with potential or existing clients, and determine the best way forward. This allows the designers and developers to focus on their projects and not get dragged into new business conversations every day. They also work very closely with project managers to make sure the team can actually deliver on what was discussed in these initial meetings. This translates into high-level requirements gathering and filtering for best fit for the company. They look for good chemistry as a whole but also for the best fit for team members.

One thing is clear from talking to hundreds of design leaders: there is no silver bullet for sales. You have to invest a lot of time in content creation to gain the awareness and credibility that more sophisticated clients are seeking in a design partner. Sales in the design business is a strategic role that's ultimately everyone's responsibility. Whether you're in a frontline job or the person sending the invoices, you will interact with the client. Every contact is an opportunity to make things better or screw things up. As far as specific new business tasks go, the ideal "salesperson" is a partner or owner of the business who is passionate about the work and the process. If your partner(s) can't be involved in the new-business process, then having domain experts that can engage in strategic conversations with prospects is the next best thing.

FINAL WORDS

Sales and marketing can be a complicated dance. In a digital world, the lines between these departments are becoming increasingly blurred. To make things more challenging, delivering on business development objectives requires finely tuned hard skills and boatloads of soft skills. The good news seems to be that these skills can be taught and improved on by almost any design leader. The critical skills are things you can't learn in a book. They are the enthusiasm and empathy that many successful great design leaders bring to the table. Meeting with dozens of these leaders was an education in itself. Even leaders with no formal sales training were bringing home opportunities using just their excitement and desire to solve clients' problems.

"I think the owner will always be the best salesperson because they not only have the passion, but they have the ability to make decisions," says Ben Jordan. "If you have someone who is passionate about the business and passionate about it moving forward and passionate about solving potential clients' problems, they're going to be good at sales." Jordan's comments are consistent with what we have experienced directly in the design industry and what we heard from successful design leaders. There's a strong link between passion for the business and sales performance. "A lot of salespeople say it, but I think it's important for people to know that they shouldn't sell things they don't believe in," says Jordan. "There is no flatter sales pipeline than someone who couldn't give a shit about what they are selling."

KEY TAKEAWAYS

- Sales and marketing can't be seen as separate activities. They are linked at every step.

- Successful design leaders think of themselves as their team's primary marketing and sales representative.

- Transparency about process, skills, challenges, and insights is now considered the norm. No more black-box methodologies and processes.

- Developing sales skills is possible for almost anyone as long as you have the enthusiasm and passion for your business.

- Sales, done correctly, is nothing more than a series of conversations about a mutually beneficial relationship and set of outcomes.

- Relying on referrals and word of mouth isn't enough. A structured lead-generation process is what drives a healthy pipeline.

- Developing a sales lens that speaks to your firm's focus and strengths ensures that sales efforts are dedicated to the right opportunities, and avoids dead-end negotiations.

- Sales is never done. Even when things are good, it's necessary to push work into the pipeline.

- Having said that, be prepared for ebbs and flows. Realize that in spite of consistent efforts, your results will vary month to month and season to season.

Learning from Our Biggest Mistakes

Introduction

It's possible that our best lessons are from the mistakes we've made. Design leaders experience them every day. Some are small and some are monumental. Many of us can't even remember all the mistakes we've made and the lessons we've learned. Some mistakes we'd rather not remember—but we've all made them. "Greg [Storey] and I did a whole workshop at Owner Camp on mistakes, so yes, we know about mistakes," says Greg Hoy of Happy Cog. "The workshop filled half a day but we probably could have filled half a week." In the past, mistakes weren't shared or discussed. Today it's a topic on blogs and at many design conferences, even if it's only discussed around the bar afterwards and not on the main stage. Fortunately for the industry, we've reached a point where design leaders are willing to share their failings and mistakes. Extreme transparency is the new normal. It's what made writing this book possible. Leaders who open up about the challenges of running a successful design group in the current technology and economic market help us all learn how to be better. We asked our leaders which hard lessons stuck out as the most memorable.

The Business Is the Design Project

As we've seen throughout these interviews, a common theme in any industry is that owners and leaders are very often the technical craftspeople who, through happenstance, find themselves running a business. Being a master of your craft doesn't translate to being a master of business. This is true of designers as well. For many of the leaders we spoke to, learning to see a business as a creative challenge was one of their biggest breakthroughs. Very often, breakthroughs happen after many years of hard work and much trial and error. For design leaders, learning the craft of running a business is more important than learning the craft of design.

"We're 15 years into this business. The 5-year mark was when I realized it took 5 years to make it work," says Warren Wilansky, founder of Plank. "So when we started the company, we had another founder. She left at about year four. When she was in the process of leaving, it became clear that up until then we were running the business like a hot potato. We were passing decisions back and forth, and neither of us was really owning anything." As the leadership structure changed, Wilanksy was forced to consider how the business was going to be run. "We both were communication graduates, and we figured we were just going to run a little company. We would just not work for somebody else and everything would just work itself out. And then when she left, I was suddenly holding the potato and I realized, okay, is this really a company? Am I going to try and run it like a company? When I got to that point and I realized that, that's when I owned it." This realization that there had been no real thought put into the company was the turning point for Plank. The next breakthrough came when Wilansky connected the dots between his skills as a designer and the way leaders need to solve problems. "I think the reason I was resistant to running a company up until that point is that I didn't see that as a creative endeavor unto itself. At that point, I suddenly realized the process of running a business was that creative project itself. So it wasn't the project in the office that I was working on. I was now working on the company as a creative project itself."

Wilansky's mistake had been to think of managing a business as something not in his skillset. After all, he was a designer and a communication major. What did he know about business? "Once I wrapped my head around it that way, that's when it became clear to me that I could actually own that and be comfortable with it. It meant that I would choose to own finance, administration, business development, and marketing." Business leadership is a design problem waiting to be solved. Creating solutions is what design does, and business is very often just a series of problems waiting to be solved. Fifty-four percent of design leaders believe that with the right guidance, designers can become business leaders. Thirty-six percent of those interviewed think that designers make great leaders.

Business leadership might be a design problem, but when our design leaders decided to start their companies, they often mentioned that it was driven by the fact that they wanted more freedom. They want the control they can't have when working for others. Sometimes being a witness to mistakes that they see in other's businesses are what drives leaders to start their own firms. "A lot of it was being on teams and recognizing people making mistakes, and you're like, 'Why are we doing it this way?' or 'Why don't we do it this other way?'" says Marty Haught, owner of Haught Codeworks, reliving the conversations he had before he started his own business. "This seems obvious to me. Is this obvious to everyone else?" After enough of those, you're like, "Okay. I can do this. I'm confident that we can do this ourselves. We'll see what happens, but I can pull it off.' Just the drive that I wanted to do it [and] feeling that I could pull it off definitely pushed me along. I'm a risk-taker, so I'm not afraid of failing or not doing as well as I'd hoped on a project."

Starting FastSpot was something of a design project for Tracey Halvorsen. The mistakes she saw working in other companies inspired her to create a new solution. "It was a little bit by mistake and a little bit by design. I have a hard time being quiet about things, which I think will accidentally propel you into a position of leadership sometimes because you're the one that's willing to take the risk. So I guess my willingness to take risks allowed me to decide that I wanted to do things better than how I saw they were being done, particularly with leading a design agency. I had a lot of great experiences with horrible companies. I was working with great people but had horrible bosses, horrible management processes, [and] horrible cultures. And I thought, 'All right, I'm going to make something better here.' So that's what got me started." This can-do attitude described by Haught and Halvorsen blends well with the business-as-a-design-problem approach. A desire for freedom might start your design studio, but it's solving problems with the design mind that keeps leaders engaged.

What can be more emblematic of good design than empathy? The model for good design almost always starts with understanding all sides of the story. Empathy as a design methodology feels tailor-made for leadership. "Leadership by empathy," says Sarah Tesla. "There are a lot of examples of successful people out there who tend to have a bit of a hard edge to them and you think, well, maybe that's how leaders should be. Sometimes you've just got to be cut and dry, and you have to give the hard feedback and that kind of thing. That has its place, but an empathetic approach goes way beyond that and earns you a different type of respect." Tesla admits that her mistake was trying to be too hard, like the traditional leader models she had read about. "I experimented with being a tough leader in the early days, and I thought, okay, I'll just be a hard-ass about this. I'd deliver my tough response to a team member and I immediately got the look from them that said, 'What the fuck are you talking about?' Like, 'Who are you right now?' I learned pretty quickly that being a hard-ass was a fail. I won't ever do that again." Approaching mistakes with empathy embodies trust and leads to insights that make the learning deeper and more inclusive.

Letting Go, Somewhat

Providing a place to be creative is one of the design leader's highest priorities. For leaders that came up through the traditional design route, it's often hard to release creative tasks to others and delegate. "There was a lot of stuff at the time about how to get creative," says Jon Lax, cofounder of the now dissolved Teehan +Lax. "Some of this was around how we would do brainstorming. In my mind, it was almost as if creativity was procedural and there was this series of steps that you could manage creativity through." Finding a process to do things is what design leaders need to do, but sometimes making those processes too regimented can backfire. "What I didn't understand at the time was that, while there are things that kind of work, what you really need to figure out as a leader is [that] it's your job to create a framework—or a place for creativity to happen—but not really to impose your will on it."

Letting go of the creative process means building a culture of trust. "I tried to impose my will on it too much, and what ended up happening was [that] I would come into a creative meeting and suck all of the oxygen out of the room. It became about dominant voices or about the process. I would say 'No, we need to do this now, and this is the step now. Let's do this game. Let's do this activity.'" What Lax told us he learned from this experience was that it's the leader's job to create a place where creativity happens, rather than a system for creativity. "What I've learned personally, and what works for the studio, is [that] it starts with having values that are very specific. You have to understand what you value, and then create a culture that values that. If you do that, creativity and ideas flourish inside of that world." The alternative to creating too much process involves a lighter touch than many leaders are willing to provide. Backing off the structure and giving the team the space to figure out the details on their own has a creative upside. "It's a much softer hand than I think I initially came in with. I thought about it as managing creativity, and then you realize that that's sort of an insane way to do it."

"My biggest mistake was not letting someone go when you know you need to let them go," says Sarah Tesla. "Oh my God, if there's anything a business owner should learn—because not letting [that person] go is the worst thing you can do—is to have to sit down and do that. Sometimes when you're starting off and you're just figuring out how this all works, and you've got someone who's just not quite fitting in or is letting the team down, or whatever, you feel like you need to be very involved." Tesla reminds us of the anxiety felt by many design leaders to overly manage situations that seem to be problematic. Developing trust that the team will figure it out might take some time, but Tesla insists that it's a skill worth learning. "You have to take care of it or else it will haunt you."

Managing Growth

Growth is part of the natural path of any successful company. In almost all cases, some type of growth is desirable—but when growth for growth's sake creeps in, mistakes happen. "In the late 1990s, I grew the company fast because of demand and because I could," says Dave Gray of XPLANE's fast and painful growth back then. Growth is the consequence of successfully delivering on value and responding to increasing demand for that value. In a service business, growth generally means adding more people. More people means more complications and more commitments. Because of this, adding people to sustain growth is a double-edged sword. If growth is your only strategy, then it lacks the fundamentals to ensure this growth is supported in both the short- and long-term.

"There have been mistakes we've made along the way," reflects Greg Hoy. "Some of the staffing decisions that we made were probably a bit ambitious, especially in terms of getting a number of people in at one time to satisfy a need that we anticipated." Hoy's story is familiar to all design studios. The promise of new projects demands consideration for who will do the work. Having the right size team for the project that's coming down the pipe is an ongoing concern for all studio owners and executives. However, it's a chicken-and-egg problem that's not easily solved. "Working in this business, you see your pipeline as one thing one day and something else two weeks later. So staffing up to support a pipeline that looks one way one week, [you'll find that] two weeks later it's something else. It's a roll of the dice. We've encountered that situation before so that's one mistake we've learned from." Hoy, who scaled up his team in anticipation of upcoming work, had the unenviable task of letting some of those people go when the work didn't get approved.

"The whole client vetting process is something that we've learned from," says Hoy. "Sometimes you'll go after the cash-cow account because you think it'll set you up for the next year or two. You're not really thinking about the warning signs that they may be displaying through[out] that process. You're going to get a paycheck but it's going to be the most painful paycheck you've ever gotten. We've had a few relationships like that, that have dragged on for years. It's because we were maybe a bit too ambitious to get that account and have that kind of security without really thinking about how it would [affect] our lives for that period of time. So I mean those are some of the bigger ones.... There's people stuff that I learn [about] on a daily basis.... I went to school for business—I didn't go to school for psychology and to know how to necessarily understand what makes people tick. I've picked a lot of that up along the way but I'm constantly making mistakes with people. I'm learning from those mistakes and trying to make sure that I don't make those in the future."

Growing pains are ongoing and are never truly put to bed. "In those first formative months, it was defining who we want to be, being able to share that story and tell it, and then research and watch and listen to see how close we were to that already," says Ben Jordan of nGen Works' recent reorganization. Jordan, who took over leadership and part ownership of nGen Works, wanted to balance the company's longstanding relationship with future expectations. To do this successfully meant developing a lens through which he could focus decisions. "We needed to see what had existed and had been done well in the past that would be worth bringing back. That required a lot of listening and asking questions. I spent time just standing back and watching what was currently going on at the company. Using this research, I was able to compare between what had gone on in the past with what people's expectations were for the future. I guess we were coming up with a framework." Once the framework was developed, Jordan was able to identify what would fit into the nGen of the future and what things wouldn't fit into that vision. Some of the insights gained required tough decisions and resulted in changes in the team. "We have had to part ways with certain people. What made it easier was [that] we had this framework. In previous leadership roles, I'd made the mistake of just running in and saying that this is the way it's supposed to be but not having anything to measure against that. People want to know how we're going to do this. They want to know why. It's a game of setting expectations. And so I think for the first time in my career, I didn't rush it. And I think that's paying off. I think people really understand what the company is doing."

The newly crafted clarity of the company vision has allowed the team to understand how to represent the company to the world outside and attend to their growth. "They are being ambassadors for the company. They are telling their friends, 'Hey you need to come work here.' We're now in that phase where people have started to inherit this new vision and inherit this new thing for themselves. Hearing them tell a new client and potential hires about these things that we were forming just three or four months ago is very exciting." Jordan acknowledges that managing the growth of the company is an ongoing task. "I think we still have a good way to go. If you are not changing, you're dying. I'm really happy with the fact that I think we are now aligned with the framework. The people know what it is. If you ask people what nGen Works is today, what we are today, they can actually answer it in a way that I agree with, and I think that's critical."

Working with Clients

Codework's Marty Haught claims to have seen his share of client-related mistakes over the years. "I didn't go to school to study business. I've learned along the way about the things you should and shouldn't do running a business. A lot of it has nothing to do with actually designing and building software. It's all about managing relationships, and sort of planning ahead, and making sure that things are covered." Haught's biggest concern is for his team. Although the team is small, he feels he needs watch their backs and provide a supportive place for them to work. "I want to make sure that my guys are covered, that they have work, that we're going in the right direction [and] we're doing enjoyable projects. There's that aspect, but there's also dealing with clients that don't have your best interest at heart sometimes. I would say that being too trusting of clients has been probably my biggest downfall. I've managed it fairly well, but I've gotten burned by people being very dishonest and almost having to go to court about things. It's like, okay, be wise about that. Make sure you understand when you're going into contracts with someone what your contract's doing for you [and] what it's not doing for you. If there are issues, how do you communicate and manage that proactively, as opposed to letting things fester and get to a point where there's really no way to win. Both sides are pretty damaged in the process. I think at this point I've learned enough that I'm avoiding that. I'm catching. I'm looking for warning signs early on and making sure it doesn't go any further because if it goes further, then it affects the team. I would rather insulate them, let them work, and keep the less pleasant aspects of working for clients away from them so it doesn't affect their work."

"The one lesson that sticks out the most is with a client that was a professional services company. We were doing great for a long time and then a dip [happened and] we hit a downturn," recalls Carl White of Think Brownstone. His team needed to deliver on the professional services project, but with a depressed market it was unclear where the cash flow would be in the near future. The market was tight and if the team wasn't able to get the project done on time, he was looking at a serious layoff of staff. In spite of this, White's client was insensitive to his expenses and couldn't understand why he might need to scale back their creative team. "I knew we couldn't afford to scale back too much because we had upcoming work. We were also working on trying to close more work, so solving this turned into a very late night," explains White. His breakthrough came when he realized he had been managing the client's expectations with the wrong information. He needed to speak to them in a language they would understand. "It was a failure because I didn't understand their leadership. They were CPAs. They were numbers guys. I knew I had to communicate to them in a way that they would understand. That was through spreadsheets and even visualizing some of those spreadsheets with charts." Delivering the right communication in the right medium had the impact that White needed. "Literally the next morning, everything changed for me. We didn't have to lay anyone off. Until I was able to speak their language, we were just another cog in the wheel. We were just another resource for them and [one] that was probably likely going to get cut." Communication skills comes up as the primary area for growth among design leaders. It seems that even veterans of the industry are still required to improve these skills on an almost daily basis.

Learning where your boundaries are as a design leader sometimes has to be learned the hard way. For design leaders running agencies, the nature of the client-agency relationship can be difficult to manage. As Marty Haught mentioned earlier, being a design leader isn't just about designing product. It's mostly about managing people and expectations. "There is all the classic stuff," remembers Greg Storey when asked about his earliest mistakes as a greenhorn designer. "I remember creating a logo for a trucking association. At their request, they wanted me to redesign their newsletter. This is before the Web, so I redesigned their quarterly newsletter and created a logo for them. I did the work and they loved the newsletter. Then they said, 'We would like the logo. How much is this? I told them $300, and they said, "Wow, we'll take the newsletter, we can't take the logo.' I made it clear, 'All right, but just so we're clear, this is now my property.'" Storey assumed that the client would take the high road and respect the intellectual property agreement that protects all design work. "I told them that it's always been my property and I retain the rights for this, [following the standard of] 'You cannot use it until you pay for it.' A couple of months later, I found out that the newsletter went out with the logo. It took guts to go after these guys by myself and say, 'You owe me 300 bucks,' you know? It took a lot of phone calls and letters, writing back and forth, but I got my money."

Communication, or specifically miscommunication, is probably the thing that causes the biggest problems in any design project. Whether it's a design agency delivering on a multimillion-dollar project or a freelancer's first job, making sure everyone is on the same page tends to be at the heart of most problems. "Let's say a lot of it has to do with communication issues," says Storey about running his design studio Airbag. "A lot of the problems—if I look back in the early years—are just communication problems. I'd say the one that I've learned, especially getting into web design, was if I was behind on the work and if I needed more time, I needed to call the client and tell them right away." Getting out in front of potential communication issues is how leaders remain successful. Being a design leader means seeking value outside of just the design work. Pushing pixels alone isn't going to solve problems. "Not burying myself in Photoshop was a big lesson. That never works. It took probably a year or two of just pissing people off in the early days of Airbag. Just pissing off clients and eventually losing a client—it took all of that pain and stress and tension until I realized that communication is more important than design in a design world."

"I think on a business ownership level, the biggest mistake I made early on was putting the client before the team and letting the client basically destroy the team," says Smallbox's Jeb Banner. "There are a couple [of] projects in particular where I should have defended our work and our people, and instead I let the client drag us around and it undermined the trust that I have with my team. I see it as my job to create a great habitat for the people that work at my companies, and in exchange their job is to create great work for those we serve, and in exchange those people pay the bills. A lot of times what happens is the leadership serves the client and the employees become the dogs, and I did some of that. That was a really good learning experience [that manifested due to] a mistake that I made. And I rarely make that mistake now. Not to say that we don't do bad work sometimes—that's different. That's us as a unit saying, 'Hey, we can do better.' But throwing my team under the bus to please the client when the client's not right—that's been a mistake that I've learned [from]." Clients, whether external or internal, are often not even aware of this dynamic. The client is making requests and the design leader is responding to them with the mindset that the customer is always right. What the design leader needs to keep in mind is that the client isn't the design expert. The client requests might be well intentioned, but they are not always well informed. This knowledge will help leaders to avoid chasing requests that are not good for project outcomes.

Making Better Mistakes

Part of good communication is decision-making. Having the confidence to make a decision and then communicate that to the team is what leadership is all about. For many leaders, those decisions are only clear when their vision is clear. "One of the big challenges that we face is that we're a husband-and-wife business," says Anthony Armendariz of Funsize about the decisions that they have to make to ensure their success. "We try really hard not to make any mistakes, because our marriage is on the line [and] our team is on the line; we've put everything into this. We just can't afford to fail. I think in the beginning, that kind of thinking actually hurt us, because we would take too long to make a decision." Realizing that slow decision-making was not making leadership easier, Armendariz and his partner used the opportunity to frame the way they wanted to work so decisions would be easier to make. Having a clear vision of how they wanted to work gave them the structure they needed to know what would fit into that vision and what would not. "Over time, thinking really hard about the business helped us figure out exactly what we wanted. What kind of space we wanted to work in, who exactly we want to work with, what kind of clients and what kind of business we should bring in that we're actually going to enjoy."

Using these mistakes as a platform for learning is the cornerstone of the Funsize success. "I think we constantly make mistakes, but we have an environment here that [allows us to] adapt and change really quickly." Says Armendariz, "Learning from those failures, it's actually been exciting to kind of fail, especially this early on. We've only been in business for a year and eight months and I feel like we've got a lot of some of the bigger pain points out of the way." Avoiding mistakes seems impossible, but getting the big ones out of the way quickly might be one strategy to aim for. This can also be achieved by learning from others. Mentors, advisors, board members, and partners are the ideal source for insight. It's never too early for young designers to find mentors.

"I think one big thing has to do with young people getting into the industry and starting out," warns Envy Labs' Jason VanLue when asked about making mistakes. "Here's the problem: one of the great things about our industry is [that] there's this sense of entrepreneurship, or individualism, or wanting to make things and wanting to create things. At least for me [when I was] getting started in the industry, there was a strong desire to just strike out on my own and 'go west' and find my territory. I would actually recommend against that for most anybody who's getting into the industry. I wish I would have gotten into a really solid firm, or agency, or group of people that I could just sit under and be an apprentice or be someone who can just glean from people." VanLue cautions against starting out on your own without all the nondesign knowledge you need as a design leader. "I didn't really know what to do, or how to write contracts, or how to deal with clients. Even today I'm still trying to figure a lot of those things out as I go. That's one big thing. I think if you're new to the industry—even if you're not necessarily young but [are] getting into the industry when you're a little bit older—find somebody who can really be a mentor to you. Find somebody who you can watch [to see] things happen and be able to get some of those experiences before you strike out on your own."

Leading a design team or business means getting guidance from others that have walked this path before you. As VanLue points out, if you're the one in charge of the team, then knowing how to write a contract might be more important than knowing design. "Learn the actual inner workings of the business," reiterates Tesla. "When it comes to money, take the time to really understand what your tools are. I got caught up in just bringing the business in and getting the work done, and then not really taking the time to understand what the tools were that were the bedrock of building the agency in the early days. And if you have that at the beginning stages, you've got a leg up. It will help enormously." This last point is at the heart of this book. Being a design leader means also being a sales leader, a finance leader, a people leader, and many more types of leader. Design leadership is multidimensional. Whether you're the founder of a small agency or head of design at an international conglomerate, your skillset can never be restricted to just the domain of design.

FINAL WORDS

Making mistakes is human. They cannot be avoided and from what we heard, it's clearly better to embrace these mistakes as learning experiences. Embracing these obstacles, and even honoring them, is by no means easy, but it is the best path forward. What separates design leaders from others is the ability to tackle life knowing full well that the mistakes will come. There's an underlying lesson in this, too. Having the courage to lead knowing that you'll face failure and disappointment is a special quality. Taking the more challenging path isn't less scary, but the rewards seem to be better. 'Don't be ashamed. Don't be shy," says Jeb Banner. "Don't be afraid to put yourself out there. Be bolder.'"

I've made my share of mistakes, but the biggest have also resulted in the best lessons learned. For me, these lessons are almost always about managing people's expectations. Not overpromising has been key to this. In the early part of my career, I wanted to please too many people. This lead to promising the world to my teams and to my clients. That spread me too thin and eventually lead to me disappointing a lot of people. The worst part is that this type of behavior also results in exhaustion and, in my case, a few days sick in bed. Even when you're in the service industry, it's best to set realistic expectations.

KEY TAKEAWAYS

- Communication problems tend to be at the root of all project problems. Getting on the same page prevents mistakes.

- Be empathetic and learn to speak your client's business language. Don't just use design jargon.

- Business is also a creative task. Approaching business like a design project can prevent mistakes and can feel more engaging for design leaders without business training.

- Mistakes can happen when decision-making powers are not clear. The buck has to stop somewhere.

- Letting go and delegating gives design leaders more freedom and time to deal with the bigger issues.

- Building trust with the team is the fastest way to delegating success.

- Don't grow for growth's sake. Being bigger for the purpose of being bigger isn't a reasonable strategy.

- Avoid mistakes by developing contracts and documentation to make project expectations clear to everyone.

- Contracts are also a great fallback when things do go wrong.

Index

H

hard and soft approaches to leadership,
  balancing, 96
hard skills and soft skills, 21
harmony versus work-life balance, 60
helping others be better at their jobs, 102
hire-your-friends approach, 17
Hollywood Model of team management,
  49, 50, 101
honesty in leadership styles, 102
hours spent working, 3

I

incentives for salespeople, 124
individualism, 144
interior designers, design leaders as, 43
internships versus apprenticeships, 31

K

knowledge or services, packaging, 86

L

layoffs, 30
layouts and interior design of office spaces,
  45
leadership, 71
  (see also personal growth and finding
    balance)
  by empathy, 137
  CEO as chief sales officer, 120
  getting guidance from others with more
    experience, 145
  growing companies by growing leaders,
    70
  importance of leaders in front-line sales
    roles, 119
  leading a design team or business, 145
  managing people and their expecta-
    tions, 142
leadership styles, 91-105
  balancing hard and soft approaches, 96
  dawing the best from others, 102
  failure as a gift, 91
  leading by connecting, 94
  long-term style, 99

many styles, one goal, 100
planning and, 76
leads
  converting to deals, 119
  origins of, 130
learned planning, 74
learning, 135
  (see also mistakes, learning from)
  failure as learning opportunity, 91
  growing skils for personal growth and
    harmony, 68
  humility and willingness to learn, 56
  learning mindset in leaders, 93
  thinking about the future, 79
learning cultures, 11
  in nurturing organizations, 9
leaving companies, reasons for, 15
legal issues with use of freelancers, 31
The Lens, 126
  creating your own sales lens, 127
  in action, 129
  putting the sales lens to use, 127
letting people go, 29, 138

M

market
  aligning planning with market realities,
    82
  connecting to market needs in plan-
    ning, 88
marketing (see sales and marketing)
meetings, 3
membership organization, 9
mentoring, 27
  demands of, 26
  finding a mentor when starting a busi-
    ness, 145
micromanagement, 92
  versus being hands-on tough, 97
  versus giving people space to work, 103
mission
  aligning marketing with, 112
  bus metaphor, 22
mistakes, learning from, 135-146
  embracing mistakes as learning experi-
    ences, 145
  letting go, 138

About the Author

Richard Banfield is the CEO and cofounder of Fresh Tilled Soil, a Boston-based product design firm. The company designs user experiences and digital products for its category leader clients. Over the last 10 years, Fresh Tilled Soil has designed and built over 600 websites, web apps, and SaaS products. Clients have included Intel, Harvard, Titleist, Constant Contact, Cigna, Rethink Robotics, Jibo, and hundreds more. *Design Leadership* is his second book published by O'Reilly. The first was *Design Sprint: A Practical Guidebook for Building Great Digital Products*, which he coauthored with C. Todd Lombardo and Trace Wax.

After completing a degree in biology, Richard was attracted to the world of web technologies and worked his way up the digital food chain, starting with online ad sales at MultiChoice, Africa's largest TV and Internet media business. He was in the thick of it during the dot-com years, cofounding Acceleration, an international advertising technology business headquartered in London (now owned by advertising giant WPP).

Richard has delivered product design, high-level business strategy, global marketing campaigns, and workshops to clients in the US, UK, Europe, and Africa. His colorful life experience includes being an officer in the South African Defense Force and being a dive master on the remote Islamic Republic of the Comoros, where he learned survival skills that he uses daily in the fast-paced tech world. Richard is a mentor at several incubators and accelerators as well as an advisor and lecturer at the Startup Institute.

Colophon

The animal on the cover of *Design Leadership* is a short-toed snake eagle (*Circaetus gallicus*). It is part of the Accipitridae family, which includes hawks and other eagles, and can be found in parts of Russia, the Middle East, Asia, and the Mediterranean. They nest in trees in semi-desert climates.

Male and female short-toed snake eagles are similar in appearance. They have brown coloring on their top plumage (head, neck, and top of the wings), but the shading can vary. The undersides are white at the lower breast and belly with brown spots or blotches. Females are heavier than their male counterparts and have longer tails. They have rounder heads than other raptors, which give them a slight resemblance to an owl.

As the name suggests, the short-toed eagle's diet relies heavily on snakes. Though they are able to eat some venomous snakes, they are not immune to poison and stick mostly to the nonvenomous variety. They are also known to eat frogs and lizards, as well as smaller birds or mammals. They hunt both while in flight or from a perch and have been known to battle prey on the ground until the target is dead and, therefore, more easily consumable.

Breeding for the short-toed snake eagle takes place during the spring months. Females will prepare the nest in trees or on cliffsides while the male provides meals for her to dine on. Females lay only one egg per mating season. Chicks typically leave the nest around two to three months after hatching, but parents will continue to provide food to the fledgling for a few weeks afterward.

Many of the animals on O'Reilly covers are endangered; all of them are important to the world. To learn more about how you can help, go to *animals.oreilly.com*.

The cover image is an animal illustration by Karen Montgomery, based on an engraving from *Lydekker's Royal Natural History*. The cover fonts are URW Typewriter and Guardian Sans. The text font is Scala Pro and the heading font is Benton Sans Condensed.

Get even more for your money.

Join the O'Reilly Community, and register the O'Reilly books you own. It's free, and you'll get:

- $4.99 ebook upgrade offer
- 40% upgrade offer on O'Reilly print books
- Membership discounts on books and events
- Free lifetime updates to ebooks and videos
- Multiple ebook formats, DRM FREE
- Participation in the O'Reilly community
- Newsletters
- Account management
- 100% Satisfaction Guarantee

Signing up is easy:

1. Go to: oreilly.com/go/register
2. Create an O'Reilly login.
3. Provide your address.
4. Register your books.

Note: English-language books only

To order books online:
oreilly.com/store

For questions about products or an order:
orders@oreilly.com

To sign up to get topic-specific email announcements and/or news about upcoming books, conferences, special offers, and new technologies:
elists@oreilly.com

For technical questions about book content:
booktech@oreilly.com

To submit new book proposals to our editors:
proposals@oreilly.com

O'Reilly books are available in multiple DRM-free ebook formats. For more information:
oreilly.com/ebooks

O'REILLY®

Have it your way.

Printed in the USA
CPSIA information can be obtained
at www.ICGtesting.com
JSHW011749120923
48355JS00016B/457